"If you are like me, you tend to gloss over your suffering, thinking it unspiritual to dwell on it. The pain is like a friend whose visit you really do not want. Paul and Dave teach us the importance of sitting with this unwelcome friend, learning from him, and, in the end, being transformed. When we do, we find we have been with the Suffering Servant whose friendship graces us in the pain, bringing us what we did not expect: peace and joy. And we find ourselves strangely warmed in the company of the saints of every age."

Scott Arbeiter, president, World Relief

"There is a deep richness that comes to people who have faced suffering biblically. A key to this richness is a joy and a contentment that tough experiences cannot take away. But many Christians do not look at suffering in this way. This book helps us to develop a theology that works in giving us the courage to look positively at suffering after experiencing the painful emotions that inevitably come with it. It does not give glib answers but faces squarely with the pain that suffering brings."

Ajith Fernando, teaching director of Youth for Christ Sri Lanka, author of *The Call to Joy and Pain*

"I've lost my husband to Alzheimer's and survived two bouts with cancer, so I read anything about suffering cautiously. *The Fellowship of the Suffering* has touched my heart and encouraged my spirit. While we all acknowledge the reality of suffering, we struggle to discover the *why*. Paul Borthwick and Dave Ripper, experienced sufferers, do not offer trite answers or slick formulas, but rather guide us to and through the *how* of the dark and disappointing days."

Cynthia Fantasia, former pastor of women's ministries at Grace Chapel, Lexington, MA

"Paul has jokingly said that this book will obviously not be a bestseller like one on health and wealth might be, but I think he's completely wrong. Suffering and brokenness are the common experiences to which all who live in this world can relate. As the authors share their stories, you will be drawn into their pain and find yourself saying, 'someone does understand.'"

Jane Overstreet, president and CEO, Development Associates International

"*The Fellowship of the Suffering* is not only biblically relevant and historically redemptive, but it's personally restorative, most notably when everything above, beneath, around, or within us seems to be falling apart. We don't realize how much we believe it to be true until we need it most. With refreshing transparency and spiritual vitality, Paul and Dave invite us to consider our broken lives in the context of the gospel of grace."

Stephen A. Macchia, founder and president of Leadership Transformations, author of *Broken and Whole*

"For many of us who are ushered down the painful path of suffering, we need a fresh reminder that as apprentices of Jesus our suffering is not a senseless dead-end, but rather a welcome mat at the open door of more intimate communion with God and others. *The Fellowship of the Suffering* lifts the myopic veil from our eyes and puts a hopeful shout in our souls as well as helpful wisdom in our hands. I recommend it."

Tom Nelson, president of Made to Flourish Pastors' Network, author of *The Economics of Neighborly Love*

"*The Fellowship of the Suffering* is an important, thorough look at all sides of suffering and our varied responses to it. There is no fluff here. Paul and Dave have worked hard to scour their own souls for how they have experienced suffering and in an honest and forthright way share their stories. A small group could study this book for a year and not run out of ideas, Scriptures, or stories to cause transformational growth and understanding that could prepare anyone for suffering well."

Gail MacDonald, author of *In His Everlasting Arms*

"So what do a couple of flourishing American Christians have to say about suffering? Quite a bit it turns out. Dave and Paul offer fresh insight into the nature and significance of suffering, drawn from thoughtful reflection on Scripture and their personal experiences with hardship and heartache. Along the way they draw upon the wisdom of spiritual masters, and share humbling and inspiring testimonies from the global church."

Bryan Wilkerson, senior pastor at Grace Chapel, Lexington, MA

"*The Fellowship of the Suffering* is a must-read. Both Dave and Paul are so open and honest about their own hardships they have suffered and remind us that we are never alone through it all. God is always with us and working in us, and we have one another to lean on."

Adam McQuaid, Boston Bruins defenseman

"*The Fellowship of the Suffering* is more than a treatise on the role of suffering in our lives. It is an *invitation*—to more deeply and profoundly experience Jesus, the community of believers, and the world that desperately needs him. No matter where you are in your journey of faith, this book will invite you to see the trials and tribulations of our lives with fresh eyes, and will offer perspective and encouragement and ultimately hope."

Manuel Luz, author of *Honest Worship*

the fellowship of the suffering

**How Hardship Shapes Us
for Ministry and Mission**

**Paul Borthwick
and Dave Ripper**

IVP Books

An imprint of InterVarsity Press
Downers Grove, Illinois

InterVarsity Press
P.O. Box 1400, Downers Grove, IL 60515-1426
ivpress.com
email@ivpress.com

InterVarsity Press® is the book-publishing division of InterVarsity Christian Fellowship/USA®, a movement of students and faculty active on campus at hundreds of universities, colleges, and schools of nursing in the United States of America, and a member movement of the International Fellowship of Evangelical Students. For information about local and regional activities, visit intervarsity.org.

All Scripture quotations, unless otherwise indicated, are taken from The Holy Bible, New International Version®, NIV®. Copyright © 1973, 1978, 1984, 2011 by Biblica, Inc.™ Used by permission of Zondervan. All rights reserved worldwide. www.zondervan.com. The "NIV" and "New International Version" are trademarks registered in the United States Patent and Trademark Office by Biblica, Inc.™

While any stories in this book are true, some names and identifying information may have been changed to protect the privacy of individuals.

Cover design: Faceout Studio
Interior design: Daniel van Loon

ISBN 978-0-8308-4530-9 (print)
ISBN 978-0-8308-8774-3 (digital)

Printed in the United States of America ♾

Library of Congress Cataloging-in-Publication Data
A catalog record for this book is available from the Library of Congress.

P	18	17	16	15	14	13	12	11	10	9	8	7	6	5	4	3	2	1
Y	33	32	31	30	29	28	27	26	25	24	23	22	21	20	19	18		

For Christie and Erin

Contents

Preface

It is by those who have suffered that the world has been advanced.

LEO TOLSTOY, QUOTED IN
WHERE IS GOD WHEN IT HURTS?

WHAT CAUSES you to suffer?

This question was posed to me (Dave) by author and professor Paul Borthwick just before we entered the Urbana 12 Student Missions Conference in St. Louis. Paul and I had been acquainted through our home church, Grace Chapel, in Lexington, Massachusetts. I serve on the pastoral staff, and Paul is a long-time member and former staff member. Though we knew each other through overlapping ministry and friendships, the depth of our conversations changed with his question. Out of our reflection on this question, our friendship has been forged in the years since.

What prompted Paul to make such a bold, pointed inquiry? It was the sermon I gave the previous Sunday on the topic of worship, a subject almost totally unrelated to personal suffering. Or so I thought. As part of Paul's feedback of the message, he said, "Even though your sermon wasn't about suffering, and you never talked about this explicitly, I felt your own personal suffering cut through your words and connect with me deeply." That's when he asked me point-blank: "Tell me, what causes you to suffer?"

Ordinarily, this would be the kind of question I would kindly dodge, using generalities, not specifics, to avoid giving a direct answer. But I decided not to do that with Paul. Why? Because I could sense a familial solidarity with him. He too was a fellow sufferer. Suffering gives birth to fellowship.

About three years later, after another sermon I preached (actually about suffering this time) titled "Suffering Comes with the Territory," Paul found me in the lobby following the service and said, "You just told me my life's story and affirmed my efforts in ministry. This is your book." Powerful words from a man who has been following Jesus longer than I've been alive and has written sixteen books! But I wasn't so sure.

A few days later we grabbed breakfast together, and Paul shared story after story, insight after insight, from all over the world, validating my instinctive sense that *the kingdom of God advances greatly through suffering*. I was floored. It became obvious to me that while I understood this pattern of God's kingdom-building activity *historically*, I simply hadn't accumulated enough experiences to notice just how significant God's work is through suffering *presently* and *globally*. I then realized this wasn't just my book, but *our* book.

Not long after that, as our prospective work got underway, it became clear that this book was even larger than just the two of us. As we shared with others about this writing endeavor, we began hearing example after example of how Christ worked through their journeys of suffering as well. We were not alone. This wasn't just a book Paul and I were coauthoring, but the very story *we*, the church, are writing. This is *your* story too. It's our story because suffering accompanies our decisions to follow Jesus Christ. It always has and, until Christ returns, always will. Suffering is as inherent to the mission of the church as the cross is to the good news of the gospel.

Following Christ in the way of the cross—no matter where, no matter what—is our history, our heritage, our story as the church.

Past, present, and future. Paul and I are merely the scribes, and like the apostle John in the book of Revelation, we are writing what we see—both in our lives, in the lives of fellow Christians around us, and in the overall history of our Christian family (see Revelation 1:10-11).

While we have collaborated on all aspects of this story-gathering, story-passing-on endeavor, at times we will either explicitly identify which of us is writing or you will be able to distinguish which of our individual voices is being heard. Paul is a boomer, a seasoned ministry veteran, missiologist, pastor, and professor who has taught and served in more countries of the world than most people can name. I am a millennial, an emerging leader, pastoring in a large church just west of Boston, rigorously learning, but still finding my way. I hope to write not only what I know, but also what I am striving to discover.

While you may be able to identify our individual voices at times throughout this book, we're prayerfully confident that only one message will emerge: God's story told in and through his church all over the world, all throughout history. A story where each of us has been given a part to play, and a responsibility for how this story unfolds. Paul and I are convinced that the story we tell will be determined by our collective willingness to suffer faithfully for the glory of God.

A Word to Those in the Throes of Suffering

Before we go any further, we imagine that many of you holding this book have picked it up because there are deep areas of suffering you're presently experiencing in your lives or in the lives of people you love. Perhaps you are feeling kicked in the gut, disoriented, or shell-shocked by a recent disappointment or turn of events. If so, you're in good company. I imagine that nearly all of us reading this have been where you are—as hard as that might seem to believe.

To help set the tone and direction for our shared journey throughout this book I (Dave) have crafted these raw, honest, hope-filled words to draw us closer together and closer to God as we begin. They are words and phrases and thoughts I've befriended throughout some of the darkest points of my journey. I hope and pray they will become welcomed companions for your journey through suffering as well.

The temptation is to believe you are the only one.
You are not.
But your suffering is unique.
No one has suffered identically to you.
So only *you* really know,
and thus your path ahead is entirely uncharted.
(Even if you're going through this with someone else.)
But we all have to cover our own uncharted territory.
This is as inescapable as the seventh grade.
Yet buried beneath is an almost-ready, waiting-to-be-
        unearthed grace
that says you can be engrafted into this uniquely same
        struggle.
(You actually already are; you're only now coming to
        awareness.)
This is the fellowship.
With me, and him, and her,
and everyone who has ever paid enough attention to notice.
For to be human—for now—is to suffer.
I, too, like you, have suffered greatly.
The experience for me, at least,
has been like a weight of clenching intensity,
followed closely behind by a full hollowness.

Like the sound your once-filled home makes
when you've just moved all the furniture out.
It's like that feeling when something is over.
Only now, you can't get over it,
no matter how hard you try.
So let me come out to say what you expect to eventually hear:
There's no way around this.
(*Why am I reading this?* you think.
Fair point. But please go on.)
A wise poet has said, "You cannot go around a desert."
How I hate him for being right.
But, oh, how I wish there was a way I could show you,
like a hidden trail only the locals know.
Oh, how I wish I could tell you that all you have to do is _____
Or just try _____ long enough
and it all will go away, and be all right, right now . . .
I can't.
But while I can't end this, I can say,
This isn't endless.
It might be days, months, years—
one can never know.
But no matter how long, there is this to remember:
This is not all there is.
This
Ache
Pain
Gnawing
Suffocating
Prostrating
Wallowing
Dying

Is

Not

All

There

Is

Mysteriously, suffering actually says that your life is *not* over.

You are *not* finished.

Why?

Because you are *worth* all this trouble.

If you weren't, you would probably just be left alone

to mindlessly coast along in life.

And where would that really get you?

According to Someone, somewhere,

You are worth this all, and all that will unfold.

There is more.

And that *more* may one day be *you* . . .

Maybe that's what's going on.

Because

Redemption always walks in your shadows,

cries in your tears,

plants in your ashes,

rises from your grave.

We don't know when.

We can't imagine how.

None of us has a clue as to why.

But you are listening to just one voice among a multitude

Who can offer assurance: You *will* make it through.

For beyond your distance lies a fellowship,

a communion who have died many little deaths,

and One death to end them all,

yet live with stains and scars and the stories to prove it.

Like pilgrims among ruins
who unfathomably possess an otherwise impossible joy.
I still can't wrap my mind around it,
but I can't shake it either.
So know: You are not alone
but are encircled by a fellowship of suffering rejoicers
who have felt unmistakably like and unlike you do,
and who have lived through enough together to agree:
Where the sufferer is, there God is.
Welcome to the Fellowship of the Suffering.[1]

PART ONE

welcome
to the
fellowship

Suffering Comes with the Territory

Contrary to what might be expected, I look back on experiences that at the time seemed especially desolating and painful with particular satisfaction. Indeed, I can say with complete truthfulness that everything I have learned in my seventy-five years in this world, everything that has truly enhanced and enlightened my existence, has been through affliction and not through happiness, whether pursued or attained. In other words, if it ever were to be possible to eliminate affliction from our earthly existence by means of some drug or other medical mumbo jumbo . . . the result would not be to make life delectable, but to make it too banal and trivial to be endurable. This, of course, is what the Cross signifies. And it is the Cross, more than anything else, that has called me inexorably to Christ.

MALCOLM MUGGERIDGE,
A TWENTIETH CENTURY TESTIMONY

SUFFERING FINDS US ALL. Every last one of us. Its forms are as varied, numerous, and unique as the very people on earth who experience its consequences. There is no getting around the reality that to be alive is to experience suffering.

But what actually is suffering? We know its causes: disease, disappointment, and death, to name a few. We know its effects: despair, distress, disillusionment, and desolation, to provide a far-from-complete list. But what is suffering in its *essence*?

For me (Paul) the person who has personally and through her writings had the greatest impact on my perspective on hardship and suffering is Elisabeth Elliot. Though many younger people don't know her story, it bears summarizing—if only to her establish her credibility related to the subject.[1]

Born into a missionary family with five siblings, Elisabeth Howard grew up a shy, awkward introvert demonstrating what we might identify today as some of the challenges of being a "Third-Culture Kid." Her first boyfriend, Jim Elliot, professed his love for her while they were students at Wheaton College, but he decided to leave her behind and go as a single man into missionary service.

Elisabeth also went to serve in Ecuador as a single woman missionary in the early 1950s. After months of translation work, all her research was destroyed by fire, a story related in her book *These Strange Ashes: Is God Still in Charge?* This was her first and earliest written reflection on suffering and disappointment.

Jim eventually pursued her, and they married. She knew Jim as a passionate man, and his zeal for Christ attracted her. She also knew that Jim and four others had set their hearts on reaching the Auca tribe (now called the Huarani, Waorani, or Waodani people) in Ecuador's eastern Amazon region. Jim and his colleagues worked for months to establish contact with these remote people. Finally they set a time to meet them.

Upon their first encounter, Jim and his colleagues were speared to death, leaving widows and single-mother families behind.[2] A year later, Elisabeth and her one-year-old daughter, Valerie, joined with a single woman missionary, Rachel Saint, to live with the Auca people.[3]

After completing her missionary service, Elisabeth Elliot (she kept Jim's surname as her pen name) married Addison Leitch, a professor at Gordon-Conwell Theological Seminary. Soon after, Dr. Leitch was diagnosed with leukemia and died after a long and painful ordeal. Her deep reflections on suffering became the subject of many books, and in the latter twentieth century Mrs. Elliot became a prominent voice of understanding and comfort related to suffering.[4] Elisabeth would later marry Lars Gren and continue writing, speaking, and hosting a radio program called "Gateway to Joy" into the early twenty-first century. She died in 2015.

If anyone has earned the right to offer a definition of suffering, Elisabeth Elliot surely has. She provides what may be the most all-encompassing, all-inclusive definition of suffering, which has helped us understand both the expanse and subjectivity of suffering: *"Suffering is having what you don't want, or wanting what you don't have."*[5]

Who on earth doesn't *have something they don't want*? Cancer or some other chronic disease. Infertility. Depression. Indebtedness. The experience of domestic abuse. Suffering as a result of systemic racism. A drug- or alcohol-addicted child. The sudden loss of a spouse. Traumatic memories of a family tragedy.

Or *want something they don't have*? A loving spouse. Reclaiming wasted years. A home in a peaceful neighborhood. Family members who follow Jesus Christ. A disabled child healed.

Who do you know who doesn't wish they could make something in their life either go away for good or appear with permanence? Ponder this for a moment yourself: What do *you* have that you don't want? What do *you* want that you don't have?

The bottom line: your personal and particular kind of suffering *counts* as suffering. Some things (like being ostracized from your family) might be specific sufferings *for* Jesus, but suffering in all forms draw us into the fellowship of those who suffer. Whatever kind of pain or suffering you're experiencing, it's real, it's acknowledged, and God stands with you and is present with you.

You suffer. We all suffer. Forgive our bluntness, but suffering—in so many forms—sucks!

Those of us who consider ourselves Christians are no exception either. In fact, we are not only included in the human experience of suffering but are given widespread biblical witness to prepare us for suffering that might have been avoided had we chosen not to follow Christ: persecution, hardship, relational turmoil, loneliness, confusion, seasons of spiritual darkness. The suffering Christians experience is as varied as the suffering all humans experience. And often just as unpredictable and every bit as painful.

The witnesses to Christian suffering seem relentless. Jesus was explicit: "If anyone would come after me, let him deny himself and take up his cross and follow me" (Matthew 16:24 ESV). "In this world you *will* have trouble" (John 16:33).

James was insistent: "Count it all joy . . . *when* you meet trials of various kinds" (James 1:2 ESV). Not *if* but *when*.

Paul was unapologetic: "There's a lot of suffering to be entered into in this world—the kind of suffering Christ takes on" (Colossians 1:24 *The Message*).

Scripture is emphatic: suffering, in all its forms, is an unequivocal, inescapable part of not only the fallen human condition but the Christian life. Given this reality, we must ask, *How can we learn to live as fully and faithfully as possible, despite the unavoidable, unwelcome presence of suffering?* This is the driving question of the book.

The Territory of Ministry

A couple of years ago my wife, Erin, planned the ultimate thirtieth birthday present for me (Dave). She arranged for us to travel from Boston to Montana to meet one of my favorite writers, Eugene Peterson, and his wife, Jan, at their home on Flathead Lake. Peterson has written close to three dozen books on spiritual theology and pastoral ministry, but is best known for his translation of the Bible, *The Message*. Pastor Pete, as many of his former congregants called him, is a pastor's pastor who has spoken most honestly about the challenges and temptations that come with pastoring in the late modern world. For those tempted to do God's work the world's way, Peterson's words resound piercingly and prophetically like a "voice calling out in the wilderness."

Over lunch Erin spoke very vulnerably about just how tough her life as both a mental-health therapist and pastor's wife can be. She described her experience as feeling like she walks around with a constant weight that's heavy, isolating, and even sickening at times. She admitted that she wasn't prepared for this—even with an excellent seminary education.

As Eugene listened compassionately to Erin's words, he leaned across the table and said something we've never forgotten. "Suffering comes with the territory." And then after a long pause, "Loneliness comes with the territory." Through the well-worn expressions on the Petersons' faces, they made it clear that behind the bestselling books and outward ministry successes were many dark, lonely, and painful seasons of life. They made no effort to pretend otherwise. To follow Jesus is to endure hardship. It doesn't matter what our role or vocational calling is, or even how outwardly successful we might seem. The same thing is true for everyone who follows Christ: suffering comes with the territory.

Accepting the Unwelcome Reality

The day we spent with the Petersons has taught us two indispensable things about living fully and faithfully in a suffering-filled world. In spite of our human desire to run from or anesthetize ourselves from hardship, we must first *accept* the reality of suffering. It comes not only with the terrain of being human but with the territory of following Christ. There is great power found in coming to terms with this. As we learn to understand that suffering will be a significant factor in our lives, suffering loses its power to take us by surprise.

Personal experience teaches us that often the more pain catches us off guard, the less capable we are of enduring it well. In other words, the pain we never see coming seems to be the hardest for us to overcome. Yet by learning to accept suffering's unwelcome presence in our lives, we can weaken its capacity to catch us by surprise. As suffering's ability to surprise us decreases, our ability to withstand hardship often increases. We see this reality forcefully at work in the life of the apostle Paul.

In several portions of Paul's writings, he outlines what have been referred to as his "catalog of afflictions" (see Romans 8:35; 1 Corinthians 4:9-13; 2 Corinthians 4:8-9; 6:4-5; 11:23-29; 12:10). These hardships included imprisonments, beatings, a stoning, three shipwrecks, hunger, thirst, nakedness, sleepless nights, anxiety for the churches, "a thorn in the flesh," and all the accompanying dangers of traveling in the ancient world. Yet despite all these horrific experiences, Paul's letters do not seem to suggest that any of these things came as a great surprise to him. He seemed ready for them. While his readiness didn't diminish the pain of such persecution and hardship, we believe it made them more endurable. His *durability* might be what enabled him to live as fully and faithfully to Christ as he did in the face of such hostile opposition.

How did Paul come to be so prepared to experience hardship? Perhaps his readiness for all the suffering he experienced in following the call of Christ came from his earliest moments as a Christian. We learn in Acts 9, during Paul's conversion to Christ, that God would "show him how much he must suffer for the sake of my name" (Acts 9:16 NRSV). While we cannot say this with total certainty, it seems possible that this vision of suffering for the sake of Jesus' name came to be something Paul not only regularly accepted but continually expected. Suffering would always accompany his ministry. If this hypothesis is true—that

Paul's readiness to suffer diminished sufferi
him—then Paul's example potently demonst
of suffering can be weakened as we come to ἑ
should be expected.

Accept the Unexpected Invitation

The second lesson we learned from the Petersons was more implicit but every bit as important. If we are first to accept the unwelcome reality of suffering in order to live more fully and faithfully, then we must accept the unexpected invitation of suffering: *fellowship*. Suffering invites us to forge a kind of fellowship we never could have cultivated any other way.

Generally speaking, when friendships and new relationships are made, they're formed out of shared interests. Both parties might enjoy hiking, a similar kind of cuisine, or fantasy literature. A new relationship then emerges and grows out of the connection between one or more of these *shared pleasures*. But as powerful as shared pleasures are for forming relationships, *shared sufferings* may be even more potent.

As Erin and I reflected on the realities of suffering that the Petersons shared with us, we felt new life breathed into our weary souls. Their sufferings validated and brought comfort to our own. Contrary to what our fears and emotions told us, we were not the only ones who faced the struggles of life and ministry that we endured. We were not the only ones who ever felt so alone. We were, in fact, in quite good company. Not merely with people we admired as profoundly as Jan and Eugene, but with many more brothers and sisters committed to following the way of Jesus in a God-dismissive world. The Petersons' counsel not only affirmed this truth for us but invited us to see new opportunities to share in this kind of relationship with others. Out of this awareness, not only *friendship* has wn between us and other fellow sufferers, but also something far greater, *fellowship*. This connection is what we are calling "the fellowship of the suffering."

Welcome to the Fellowship

The fellowship of the suffering identifies the new bonds of communion forged out of the crucible of suffering. Scripture—particularly Paul's writings—seem to indicate that there is an interconnected, paradoxical relationship between suffering and fellowship.[6] For instance, in Romans 8:17, Paul writes that if "we *suffer with* him [Christ]," then "we may also be glorified with him" (NRSV; italics added). The words *suffer with* in Greek are a form of the word *sympaschō*, which combines two words: *syn*, meaning "together," and *paschō*, meaning "suffer." It's a word unique in Scripture to Paul and connotes the idea of "sharing suffering together." Thus for Paul, suffering and fellowship can coincide harmoniously, however disparate they may at first seem. When fellowship is forged out of suffering, it creates a kingdom-advancing communion that offers everyone who suffers the opportunity to live more fully and faithfully. This communion fosters fellowship in the three most fundamental realms of relationship in our lives: (1) fellowship with Christ, (2) fellowship with others, and (3) fellowship with the world.

Fellowship with Christ

While we are never given an explanation as to why God allows such terrible suffering to occur in our world, we are given a God who suffers—a God who suffers *for us*. He "took up our pain" and "bore our suffering" by willingly subjecting himself to being "pierced for our transgressions" and "crushed for our iniquities" on the cross (Isaiah 53:4-5). Unfathomably, God the Father allowed excruciating pain and suffering to be experienced by Jesus, God the beloved Son, in inexplicable ways: "It was the Lord's will to *crush him* and *cause him* to suffer" (Isaiah 53:10; italics added). The God who created us is a God "of suffering," one "familiar with pain" (Isaiah 53:3). This God invites us to share our sufferings with him. He will not give us pat answers when we come to him; he will give us himself.

In his letter to the Philippians the apostle Paul models for us how we might accept suffering's unexpected invitation to share fellowship with God: "I want to know Christ and the power of his resurrection and the sharing of his sufferings by becoming like him in his death, if somehow I may attain the resurrection from the dead" (Philippians 3:10-11 NRSV). Often the interpretive temptation with this verse is to believe Paul is seeking to know three things: (1) Christ, (2) the power of the resurrection, and, as the American Standard Version translates it, (3) "the fellowship of his sufferings." None of us, if we're being honest, really wants to suffer, so we opt to pursue knowing Christ himself and the power of his resurrection, while conveniently leaving out or forgetting the suffering part. Our cross-stitched pillows and mass-produced scriptural artwork prove it. They merely read, "I want to know Christ"—Philippians 3:10.

The omitted parts may be the most glaring absence in the lives of Christians today—ourselves included.

Almost certainly, though, Paul is not resolving to know three things, but one—namely, Jesus—spelled out in two distinct ways. Essential to knowing Christ is knowing "the power of his resurrection." Because he has conquered death, his resurrection guarantees the resurrection of all who trust in him. Without knowing the power of Christ's resurrection and the promise of our resurrection in him, our present sufferings would be senselessly harsh and unbearable. Our hope would be in vain. Therefore, in our efforts to know Christ personally, it is paramount that we study closely and remind ourselves continually of the strength inherent in Jesus' death-conquering resurrection.

But while we can almost hear ourselves declaring wholeheartedly alongside Paul, "I want to know Christ and the power of his resurrection," we cannot stop there. We must also soberly and courageously continue along in the resolution "I want to know Christ . . . and the fellowship of his sufferings by becoming like him in his death." For apart from sharing in his sufferings, we'll only pursue knowing Christ partially, not fully. That omission will not only impoverish our faith individually but diminish our witness collectively. Thus, we must pursue knowing Christ not only as our resurrected King, but as our suffering Servant.

Part two of this book is devoted to this very effort. We enter into fellowship with our suffering God by first sharing our struggles and pain openly and honestly with him. After all, he is the only one who truly can identify with whatever we're going through. In chapter four we'll explore ways to pray to God—even when we don't want to—in order that we might cultivate an intimate and unbreakable solidarity with him.

Knowing Christ through the fellowship of his sufferings will undoubtedly have a transformative effect on our character. We will "become like him in his death," as we pursue communion with him in fellowship and prayer. In chapter five, we'll explore more thoroughly just how our hardships form our character for ministry and mission by giving our lives cruciform shape. Particularly, we'll discover how the process of being conformed to Christ in his death is a central way in which we can reach one of the primary goals of the Christian life: reflecting the image of the suffering Christ.

Accompanying this kind of cross-like transformation in our character is a pervasive and undeniable *joy*. In chapter six, we'll consider how joy is mysteriously compatible with even our worst suffering. Even though everything in our lives might not be okay, through fellowship with Christ we remain okay.

To summarize: the fellowship of the suffering is first of all—foundationally and indispensably—fellowship with our suffering Servant and resurrected King, Jesus Christ.

Fellowship with Others

The second aspect of the fellowship of the suffering, deriving from the first, is fellowship with others. Our suffering God not only invites us to share in communion with him through our suffering, but to enter into solidarity with his people, his body—the church. There are both helpful and hurtful ways to go about this.

The name most synonymous with suffering in the Scriptures is Job. He lived a good life and grew well-accustomed to living a blessing-filled lifestyle. Yet all of that changed in an instant when he learned that his wealth and family had been wiped out. His livestock, gone. His children, killed. To add still another layer of suffering atop these tragedies, Job's body was afflicted with a horrific case of boils. Enter Job's so-called friends: Eliphaz, Bildad, and Zophar.

These friends get off to a wise start in attempting to bring consolation to Job by simply sitting with him in silence for seven days and nights. After this, Job breaks the silence by cursing the day he was born. This first word spoken by Job opens the door for his friends to try to have the last word about why he is suffering and what he should do about it. Things go downhill fast from here. However noble their intentions, the friends' unsolicited counsel is a prime example of "when helping hurts."[7]

Eliphaz conclusively tells Job with prophetic confidence that his suffering is evidence of his sin. There is a clear-cut case of cause and effect going on here. Job sinned, thus Job suffers. What other explanation could there be? Shockingly, Job doesn't find this overly reassuring or helpful.

Bildad takes a different approach. He essentially contends that in comparison to the greatness of God, Job is pretty insignificant (Job 25:5-6). Who does Job think he is to expect an explanation from the God of the universe? While Bildad rightly magnifies God in his exhortation, he wrongly minimizes the people God made in his image, by surmising that God doesn't have time for them. Even though some of what Bildad communicates has theological truth behind it, the cruelly impersonal way he shares this message chokes out any of the life found within it. What Job needs isn't solution but understanding.

The third friend, Zophar, doesn't do much better than Eliphaz or Bildad. Instead of listening to Job or empathizing with his plight, Zophar pushes Job toward good works. He counsels Job, "If you direct your heart rightly . . . your life will be brighter than the noonday" (Job 11:13, 17 NRSV). In other words, to solve his problems, Job must do good deeds.

Given these "friendly" interventions, is it any wonder that Job concludes that Eliphaz, Bildad, and Zophar are "worthless physicians" and "miserable comforters" (Job 13:4; 16:2 NRSV)? In Job's time of crisis his immediate need was not for the *solution* to his problems but for *solidarity* amidst his suffering. His friends' attempts at comforting Job are helpful at least in showing us how not to attempt fellowship with those who suffer.

In contrast to this, the apostle Paul offers us a more loving way to help those who are hurting. In likening the church to the body of Christ, he writes in 1 Corinthians 12:26, "If one member suffers, all suffer together with it; if one member is honored, all rejoice together with it" (NRSV). The same word used to describe our fellowship with Christ's sufferings in Romans 8:17, *sympaschō*, is used here to describe how we are to suffer together as members of one body, the church. Just as we can pursue living fully and faithfully by seeking fellowship with Christ in our times of suffering, so we can cultivate fellowship with the body of Christ by learning to share our afflictions with one another. To do this we must be both available to others when they suffer and vulnerable about our own sufferings with others. As we do this, our unwelcome sufferings can produce unexpected fellowship with others like we've never experienced before.

In part three of this book, we'll explore this dynamic more fully by examining how solidarity within the church is birthed out of adversity. This will be the primary focus of chapter seven. Then, in chapter eight, we'll discover how this kind of fellowship formed within the body of Christ can be extended to those outside the walls of our churches, including our neighbors, coworkers, and friends. We'll contend that in our suffering-filled world pain can become the new common ground in which faith conversations empathetically emerge.

Fellowship with the World

The third realm of relationship that suffering invites us into is fellowship with the world. We haven't been welcomed into fellowship with Christ and with his church just so we may be strengthened individually, but so that we may, in turn, bring strength, hope, and healing to our broken and hurting world. God's purpose in giving our lives cruciform shape—through fellowship with him and his church—is so we may extend the work of the cross to all people and all systems in our world in desperate need of the touch of his presence. This work is anything but easy. If we endeavor to combat the sufferings of the world—injustice and isolation, poverty and persecution, sin, disease and death—then it should come as no surprise that we often will share in the effects of these sufferings ourselves. As the Petersons communicated so gently yet with forceful clarity, suffering comes with the territory of Christ's call to ministry. This call is not merely reserved for those with full-time vocational positions of missionary, evangelist, or pastor, but for everyone who follows Christ.

The apostle Paul makes this sobering reality clear in his letter to the Colossians. His intent was not to intimidate the Colossians or to scare them off, but to embolden them, and us, through the power of the Spirit to pick up the work that Christ has left for us to do. Christ's work is to be continued in the same manner in which it began. Christian work is inescapably cross work.

Paul lays out the target his ministry is aimed at in Colossians 1:28-29. "It is he [Christ] whom we proclaim, warning everyone and teaching everyone in all wisdom, so that we may present everyone mature in Christ. For this I toil and struggle with all the energy that he powerfully inspires within me" (NRSV). The goal behind all of Paul's proclaiming, warning, and teaching, is that everyone—yes, everyone!—may be fully mature in Christ. This work of evangelism and discipleship wasn't all adrenaline and adventure for Paul, but toil and struggle. To toil is to be weary, to beat one's self out with hard labor. To struggle is to fight resiliently, like a competitor in the public games, where the stakes are often a matter of life or death.

In using this kind of markedly stern language, Paul makes no effort to hide just how arduous the labor of a Christian can be. Ministry doesn't happen easily. Serving Christ leaves scars. Loving others can throw our lives in disarray. Choosing to live on mission for Jesus means committing oneself to being willing to suffer. If we truly desire to know Christ, then we too will become intimately familiar with sufferings like his.

This reality is not only what Paul wants to warn the Colossians about, but what he invites them to enter into. A few verses earlier in the letter, he boldly states, "Now I rejoice in what I am suffering for you, and I fill up in my flesh what is still lacking in regard to Christ's afflictions, for the sake of his body, which is the church" (Colossians 1:24). For many, this is one of the most perplexing statements in the entire New Testament. Is Paul really suggesting that Christ's finished work on the cross is somehow incomplete? Although at first glance it may appear that way, the answer is a definitive no. Christ's atoning sacrifice is fully sufficient for salvation, as Paul argued vigorously throughout his writings (see Romans 3:21-26; 2 Corinthians 5:16-21). What, then, does Paul mean?

Many commentators largely agree that the aspect of Christ's work that is "lacking," according to Paul, which he endeavors to "fill up in his flesh," is the *knowledge* of Christ's sufferings. In other words, Christ's sufferings in and of themselves were absolutely complete in their ability to forgive us from our sins and set us free for life with God forever. Yet, at the same time, the worldwide spread of this knowledge was far from finished. Paul is thus contending that while his sufferings are not *redemptive* in the sense that Christ's were, his hardships are *missionary* in nature. His sufferings complete what is "lacking" in Christ's afflictions in the sense that his ministry *extends* the knowledge and reality of the cross of Christ to the wider Gentile world.[8] Paul's sufferings, through the work of the Spirit, spread the knowledge and power of Christ's sufferings to those who have not yet heard or fully understood.

Earlier we quoted Peterson's translation of this passage, and it bears repeating for how well it captures both the sense and the invitation behind Paul's perplexing statement. "There's a lot of suffering to be entered into in this world—the kind of suffering Christ takes on. I welcome the chance to take my share in the church's part of that suffering. When I became a servant in this church, I experienced this suffering as a sheer gift, God's way of helping me serve you, laying out the whole truth" (Colossians 1:24-25 *The*

Message). Why did Paul "welcome the chance" to take part in the suffering Christ left the church to do? Because the suffering Paul experienced on behalf of the church enabled him to reveal "the whole truth" of the gospel to many people who had never heard it. Just as Paul entered into the "kind of suffering Christ takes on," so we are called by God to do the same. As we do so, the potential to heal the world's hurt with the love of Christ grows exponentially.

In his acclaimed work *The Cross of Christ,* John Stott boldly declares, "The greatest single secret of evangelistic or missionary effectiveness is the willingness to suffer and die."[9] We'll unpack this bold thesis offered by Stott more fully in chapter nine, as we trace the history of how suffering has advanced the mission of God. Finally, in chapter ten, we'll uncover how each of us can take our place and do our part to cultivate fellowship with the world as we raise the question, Are you *really* passionate? We'll see that the world's definition of *passion* is most often a far cry from the kind of passion Christ calls us to exhibit. Overall, we'll begin to see that not only do we "know Christ" by "becoming like him in his death," but we also *make Christ known* by living cross-shaped lives that *take on* and even *take in* the sufferings of our world.

Our Vision and Hope

Throughout this book, we hope that you discover how *God's kingdom has the potential to advance greatly as we strive to live as fully and faithfully as we possibly can, despite the unwelcome presence of suffering in our lives.* His kingdom advances in us in spiritually transformative ways as we experience fellowship with our suffering Savior. It advances through us as we share our lives with our broken and hurting neighbors and world. It advances between us to forge a fellowship of the suffering—the church—given by God to be poured out as an offering to our suffering world.

The reason we believe God's kingdom can be powerfully advanced through a fellowship of the suffering is because, as Dietrich Bonhoeffer contends, "within the fellowship of Christ's sufferings, *suffering is overcome by suffering*, and becomes the way to communion with God."[10] We believe he means that *the suffering caused by evil is overcome by the suffering inspired by cross-like love*. In other words, the suffering our human community experiences has the potential to be gradually healed through connection to a fellowship of sufferers who are experiencing healing through fellowship with our Lord Jesus Christ, the suffering Servant. Thus, we are convinced that the more the church takes its rightful place as a fellowship of the suffering, the greater hope our suffering world has for redemption.

In chapters two and three, we'll share our stories of suffering and the imperfect attempts we've made to live as fully and faithfully as possible in the midst of these hardships. Our intent is not to put our lives on the pedestal of faithful suffering, but to invite all fellow sufferers into greater communion with Christ, his church, and the world.

The Fellowship of the Ring

During the early stages of writing and researching this project, I (Dave) spent many evenings reading aloud *The Lord of the Rings* trilogy with my wife. I found myself so swept up in the plot of these treasured stories that throughout the day I often thought *I* was on assignment, alongside Frodo and Sam, Merry and Pippin, Legolas and Gimli (I'm sure Gimli would have protested the ordering of names here!), and Gandalf and Aragorn, to save Middle Earth. What particularly struck me in reading these stories was how their hardships became the vehicles that propelled them further and further toward their goal. If they tried to avoid experiencing pain, they'd risk compromising their entire mission.

Thus to destroy the One Ring in the fires of Mount Doom, they would have to leave behind their beloved homeland, sacrifice Middle Earthly comforts, resist alluring temptations, face their own fallenness, overcome their worst fears, traverse dangerous terrains, mourn the loss of trusted friends, fight battle after seemingly impossible battle, and risk their lives, only to have to risk them again and again. The only way this could be done was *together*. This group of unlikely compatriots was no mere "fellowship of the ring," but a fellowship of the *suffer*-ing.

No matter how unsettling the prospect of the fellowship of the suffering may seem, just like the fellowship of the ring we serve too great of a mission, under too great of a Savior, not to put everything obediently on the line as well.

Jesus is worth it.

Forging Fellowship Reflections

At the end of each chapter, you will find questions to reflect on personally and to discuss with others as a group. In offering these questions we hope that you and the people in your small group, church, or family will be able to take steps toward becoming more of a fellowship of the suffering together. Ask God to give you the courage, the grace, and the patience to be available, vulnerable, and present with one another—and the Spirit—in these conversations.

1. Elisabeth Elliot contends, "Suffering is having what you don't want, or wanting what you don't have." How do you suffer? As much as you're comfortable, consider sharing one thing you have that you don't want or one thing you don't have that you want.

2. Throughout this chapter the authors emphasized that suffering comes with the territory of following Christ. Describe a time when

your life was negatively impacted, or when you have experienced suffering for living as a follower of Christ.

3. The driving question of this book is, How can we learn to live as fully and faithfully as possible despite the unavoidable, unwelcome presence of suffering? How have you tried to live as fully and faithfully as possible despite the unwanted presence of suffering in your life (regardless of whether you were successful)?

4. The authors contend that the unexpected invitation of suffering is fellowship. Describe a time when the disappointments you experienced enabled you to draw closer to Christ and others.

The Worst Suffering

Paul's Story

Our tragedies can be a very bad chapter in a very good book.

JERRY SITTSER, *A GRACE DISGUISED*

IN A COURSE I (Paul) formerly taught at Gordon College titled "Global Issues Facing the Global Church," we covered a myriad of issues over the semester—refugees, world hunger, infant mortality rates, sex trafficking, HIV/AIDS, human slavery, Christian persecution, and more. Through our fifteen weeks of classes, we would read, listen to, and watch stories of an extensive array of pain and suffering in the world and then look for ways to respond.

To start the discussion in one of the earliest classes, I asked this question, "What, in your opinion, is the worst suffering in the whole world?" Students would take guesses: Hunger? Living in chronic fear? Spiritual lostness? Abandonment? Mistreatment of women? These and many more responses came—all of them good and serious identification of forms of human suffering.

But my answer surprised students. I told them, "The worst suffering in the whole world is *my* suffering." If I have a migraine headache, I'm thinking about my pain, and at that moment I am not thinking about sex-trafficked girls in Bangkok. If my teenager has run away from home, I'm probably not praying or caring at that moment about one million homeless people in some Indian city.

And if my boss delivers the news that I've been laid off, I'm most likely not worrying about the unemployment rate provoking frustration in Palestinian young people. The subjective and self-experienced nature of suffering challenges us all in two ways. First, it challenges our choices. In the face of all of our various degrees of suffering, will we make the choice to go beyond our pain to care for others, choose joy, go deeper in prayer, and more? Like Jesus on the cross, we freely acknowledge our own pain, but then we choose to care for those around us too.[1]

The second challenge is comparison. Inevitably, you probably have personal pain that motivates your interest in reading this book. As a result, you might be asking if the authors have suffered enough to be credible sources of comfort or direction. As we'll explain, we both have some experience with chronic and incurable diseases. We both know some relational pain. We both know what it is to experience the helplessness of being unable to solve the pain of seeing loved ones suffer.

The intensity of suffering and our ability to faithfully endure it is impossible to measure. For the ten-year-old who lost his favorite teddy bear, the tears of agonizing loss may flow for days (we can even say that his loss is un*bear*able). To the eighteen-year-old who just received news of a love interest dating someone else, the suffering seems unhealable. But to the person going through her third round of chemotherapy, or the married couple who cries themselves to sleep because of childlessness, the sufferings of the ten-year-old or the teenager seem incredibly trite.

This subjective nature of suffering underscores the two biggest dangers of writing a book about embracing suffering. First, you may decide that neither of us have suffered enough to be credible. Indeed neither of us has (as yet) suffered personally with cancer. Christie and I (Paul) had rocks thrown at us on a visit into Taliban-controlled

Afghanistan, but neither of us authors has experienced anything like persecution, torture, or imprisonment. We've not been disfigured in a fire, abused by our parents, or paralyzed by a fall. Have we suffered enough? You will need to decide this.

The second danger in writing a book on embracing suffering is that we might sound like we've actually succeeded in this long-term struggle. Our colleague Stephen Macchia cautioned us: "Writing a book on embracing suffering is like writing a book on humility: you'll either come across as prideful (as in 'We've achieved this') or you'll come across as trite or superficial (as in 'Ten Easy Ways to Overcome Suffering')."

We don't want either extreme. We want you to know that we are very much in process ourselves, "not having already obtained this" but rather "pressing forward"—as Paul the apostle, the most frequently quoted author in our book, writes in Philippians 3. A doctor's appointment for either the Borthwicks or the Rippers that shows further damage in our respective chronic diseases could result in more tears, deep discouragement, or even depression. We want you to know that we've sought professional counseling for grief and loss and the chronic issues of unresolved family challenges. Some days our hurts or sufferings do have dominion over us (something you'll read about later).

Bottom line: we are processing what it means to stay faithful through suffering because it's part of both our human condition and our decisions to follow a crucified Savior who calls us to take up our crosses daily to follow him (Luke 9:23).

We write all this to introduce our own subjective stories of hardships, pain, and suffering that have come our way. We'll do this in an interview format in this chapter and the next. Dave will interview Paul first. Then Paul will introduce you to Dave and Erin. We offer our stories in hopes that you will be able to share your stories with others and even with God. Stories encourage us to know that we're not alone and that God is taking us through them all. Stories fan the flames of fellowship.

Dave. Paul, can you start by telling us about your life and work now?

Paul. I'll start by stating that (at this writing) I'm sixty-three years old—a fact that bears mentioning only because some of my "sufferings" are simply related to aging. Christie and I are married thirty-eight years, and we serve on the staff of an international leadership development ministry called Development Associates International (DAI).

Dave. Many stories of your travels appear in our book, and these experiences have obviously shaped both your worldview and your views on suffering. How have these come about?

Paul. These trips to what we now call the Majority World (mostly Africa, Asia, and Latin America) started when we led youth short-term mission trips. Then I served as a missions pastor for fifteen years, and most recently the work with DAI takes us out of the country two to three months each year.

Dave. Introduce us to suffering in your own life.

Paul. I remember being a sickly child—mostly due to intestinal issues related to nerves, I think. I was in the hospital once or twice before age ten, but mostly I remember my fears of loneliness. Then my teen years launched me fast forward to physical pain—I was sickness prone and accident prone. Looking back, I think my parents (now deceased) deserve an award of some sort for getting me through the teen years. When I was between twelve and seventeen, I think they had the emergency room on speed dial.

Dave. Can you fill in some details?

Paul. At age twelve a stomach virus turned out to be undiagnosed appendicitis. The appendix burst and resulted in emergency surgery and a couple of days of what hospitals used to call "the danger list"—that is, patients in potentially life-threatening situations. A life-saving abdominal drain rid my body of the ruptured appendix fluids, but this resulted in hernia surgery six or eight weeks later.

Dave. And then?

Paul. At age thirteen I broke my left leg playing football. A guy 100 pounds bigger than me tackled me on a concrete floor. Seven weeks in a cast and on crutches. This was followed by a chipped heel bone on the same leg—two more weeks on crutches.

Dave. Football . . . on a concrete floor . . . with a guy 100 pounds bigger than you? Is this suffering or just being a foolish thirteen-year-old?

Paul. I know you're being facetious, but it's actually an important question. Some of my sufferings were caused by doing foolish things.[2] My next chapters were either an accident or carelessness: at age fourteen, while using an old-style snow blower to clear our driveway, I was brushing snow off of the top of the machine while it was running. An uncovered chain caught my glove and pulled my left hand into the sprocket. I lost the top joint of my index and middle fingers. The accident resulted in hand surgery, skin grafts, and multiple stitches (and the end of my guitar-playing career!). A year later I put my arm through a window and pulled it back quickly—resulting in a twenty-three-stitch gash.

Dave. And this is all by age fifteen?

Paul. And I'm not done yet! I managed to get through my junior year of high school relatively unscathed, but I ended my employment in my seventeenth summer when I, on my three-speed bike, collided with a driver who had jumped the stop sign. This resulted in a compound fractured right wrist and a severe concussion that left me with a damaged eye muscle and three years of double vision.

Dave. Where was your Christian faith in all this?

Paul. At age seventeen, I committed my life to Christ. The youth leader had several of us new Christians in a small discipleship group. We were reading books like Dietrich Bonhoeffer's *The Cost of Discipleship*, so I had already memorized things like "When Jesus calls a man, he bids him 'Come and die.'" But looking back on it, I don't think I had any idea what this meant. Nevertheless, in my emerging faith, I was starting to see these various sufferings through the lens of his work in my life.

The broken wrist from the bicycle accident served two purposes. It answered the question of whether I should rejoin the football team (as a new Christian, I wanted to reach out to my friends but knew that the football team environment would be tough on my newfound faith). The wrist cast also provided the answer to my prayer of how to tell my friends of my conversion: fellow members of the youth group wrote JESUS SAVES in two-inch block letters on my cast. This was my discussion starter as school resumed.

Dave. You went through a lot for a high school student, especially as a new Christian!

Paul. Actually, my high school story was not yet over. Nine days after the wrist cast was removed, I joined several other church youth group kids for a trip to a birthday party. It was the second Sunday of October; our autumn leaves had already started to fall, and it was a rainy night. We hit a patch of leaves on a curvy back road and slid at forty or fifty miles per hour into a tree. I was in the right front seat. No seatbelts, no airbags: it was 1971.

   Others were severely injured, but I got it the worst. Broken right leg in three places. Broken right and left pelvis. Assorted cuts. Torn muscles in my neck and chest. And a ruptured spleen—the injury that would again put me on the danger list, this time for ten days.

   Miraculously, I and all the others in the car survived. I had a splenectomy, received seven blood transfusions, and laid in neck, pelvis, and leg traction for a little over five weeks. Full recovery took closer to six months.

Dave. As a less-than-one-year-old Christian, how did you process this?

Paul. It was this accident that first got me thinking about the role of suffering as it relates to growth in my Christian life. In the years that followed, I memorized many of the verses that relate to suffering and growth, verses that will appear and reappear throughout the book. In one sense, this accident—the experience of physical pain, questioning "Why God?" and my distinct sense that God had saved my life—has shaped me deeply.

Dave. Is this it for your suffering résumé?

Paul. As a foundation for my later life, I suppose the answer is yes. Physical hardships subsided through my twenties until age thirty-six, when I ruptured my Achilles tendon playing basketball. The surgery and long recovery were arduous, but the doctor's comment—"This injury is very common among *men your age*"—previewed the challenges of the years ahead. Aging—the chronic disease that affects us all—was starting to reveal itself.

Dave. Speaking of chronic diseases, you refer to living with a chronic disease, but you've not told us anything about it yet.

Paul. At age forty, I was diagnosed with Type 1 (insulin-dependent) diabetes—often called "juvenile diabetes." (Christie later joked that I got a juvenile disease at forty because of my immaturity.) This diagnosis became a new life shaper, or better, a new lifestyle shaper. Injections, constant blood-sugar monitoring, and never-being-able-to-eat-food-without-thinking-about-it-first entered my life. Like a dysfunctional conjoined twin brother, diabetes went everywhere I went, and the best I could hope for was that he wouldn't act out or do something stupid.

Dave. And then?

Paul. The diabetes lifestyle alteration was overshadowed two years later by a ruptured disk in my back (more on this later), and other age-related maladies are now upon me, rendering it necessary to manage arthritis and monitor things like blood pressure and cholesterol.

Dave. Can you articulate any sort of testimony about where pain or sickness has fit in your life?

Paul. Physical suffering has tested my endurance, developed my stamina, and increased my spirit of resilience. Living with diabetes has made me more disciplined and at the same time tolerant of inconvenience. (Christie says that I have a high tolerance for physical pain too.) And being twice on the "danger list" has served as a constant reminder that every day of life is a gift from God.

Dave. From our conversations and from working together on this book, I know that you've given a lot of thought to the issue of suffering and hardship as part of the life of faith. Do you have a perspective on why we often want to run away from reflecting on the realities of suffering?

Paul. First, we need to realize that suffering is nothing that we'd choose. Even Jesus, when facing the cross, asked God the Father if there was another way (Luke 22:42-44). When facing hardship, Christie and I sometimes remind ourselves of the reality that "comfort comes naturally but suffering takes some getting used to."

Second, I think we're afraid to face the hardships of life. We all want comfort, a long life, and financial security. Wrestling with Philip Yancey's question "Where is God when it hurts?" is itself painful. It forces us to realize that God might not answer our *why* questions. As a young believer, I found myself asking a question that reflected my cause-effect assumption about hardships: "What did I ever do to deserve this?" The kind of questions that Job's friends asked him represents our fear to enter into the mysteries of suffering.

Third, our addiction to comfort and convenience often keeps us from wanting to face the realities of pain, whether our own pain or that of others. I'd love to believe that if I follow the formulas presented by the so-called prosperity preachers, suffering would no longer be part of my life.[3] But the Bible's teaching, the experiences of the persecuted church through the ages, and the example of the Lord Jesus Christ do not bear this out.

Sadly, I've seen the harm of such teaching in my own family. My dad was a devoted Christ-follower who suffered from a variety of maladies, including excruciating back pain from a ruptured disk that was never repaired. He came under the influence of a radio preacher who boldly taught that if anyone had faith enough, healing would follow, and if healing did not follow, it meant that the person either didn't have enough faith or that they had some hidden unconfessed sin. In other words, if you're suffering, it's your own fault. My dad lived in pain and went to his grave wondering what sin he had failed to find and confess.

In contrast to the biblical teaching that to know Christ means both the power of the resurrection and the fellowship of sharing in his sufferings (Philippians 3:10), the message of the prosperity gospel reduces the Christian life to a neatly packaged, simple, problem-free way to live. Just follow the formula; everything will be all right. Mystery, paradox, and pain are considered exceptions, never a normal, expected part of following Christ.

Dave. Would you say that physical suffering is your primary experience leading to your interest in and study of this topic?

Paul. Yes and no. Much of my life has been shaped by disease, accidents, and surgeries, but as husband and wife, Christie and I have experienced more in the realm of relational and emotional suffering. (Although you'll read later how her ownership of living with diabetes has deeply encouraged me.) We went on our first date over forty years ago, and we'll soon approach forty years married. Gratefully, our emotional and relational pain has not been primarily with each other but with the families we both married into.

Dave. Can you explain?

Paul. Though we have never had our own biological children, we did extensive parental-type care for aging parents (all deceased now), a mentally ill brother, and a mentally handicapped sister, and dealt with the repercussions of alcoholism in the family. Christie's favorite brother died suddenly at age forty-seven and her father died seven weeks later. Her other brother died thirteen years later on Christmas Day. And any reader who has been involved with post-death family matters knows that each of these cases has had its own challenges regarding finances, estates, wills, and more.

We've shared together the emotional pain of praying and waiting for loved ones to come to faith in Jesus Christ, but this waiting has built perseverance. Caring for the pains and problems of others that we did not create has fueled compassion. And understanding our own family pain has left us empathetic toward other families in need.

Dave. Your story contains a lot of grief, loss, and, for lack of a better way to say it, emotional pain management. What advice would you give to others in these types of pain?

Paul. First, there are no easy answers. Pain and loss and grief do not suddenly go away and you wake up and say, "Oh, I'm so glad I learned that!" Sometimes there's no clear word or explanation from the Lord—in spite of the well-meaning simplistic encouragements that other Christians give. When Christie's favorite brother and her father died within seven weeks of each other, she would sit for hours in our wing chair, what we came to call the "prayer chair," and wait, weep, and wonder what God was doing. It was her darkest night of the soul. She consoled herself with the belief that God loved her and that his character is good, but he seemed silent.

When a Christian at church cheerfully asked her, "What do you think God is teaching you?" Christie replied, "I have no idea." Sometimes the pain and losses and long-term grieving in life have caused us to repeat the words of the disciples in John 6. When presented with the costly challenges of following Jesus, they replied, "Lord, to whom shall we go? You have the words of eternal life."

I would urge readers to remember that our words in this book reflect the painful, sometimes mysterious, and never-rapid choice to choose faithfulness in the face of suffering; it is a process. And this process is not just a matter of inspirational quotations or Scripture references. It is the deep work of God's Spirit to help make us into the cross-bearing, hope-filled image of Christ.

Dave. Wow. Heavy and honest stuff. With all of the personal challenges you've faced, how have the various ministry positions you've held—and the human suffering that these have exposed you to—affected you?

Paul. Although Christie is a professional medical technologist in a microbiology lab, we both have been involved in people care through professional Christian ministry since we were married. Twenty-two years on the staff of a large church brought us into the pain and suffering of others: children killed in car accidents or from leukemia, young adults suffering from the effects of an abusive parent, loved ones dying from Alzheimer's, unfaithful spouses, rebellious teenagers, postpartum depression and subsequent suicide, a college student drowning. I've performed marriages, and some have ended in divorce. We've been called to enter many other people's pain.

More recently, our work with an international leadership organization has taken us deeper into global suffering: children dying of preventable diseases; refugees now homeless, having lost everything; persecution; political turmoil; and unjust governments.

Dave. How has seeing all this pain affected you?

Paul. The deepest result of this exposure to the suffering of others is prayer. We are constantly reminded that these issues are bigger than us, so we bring them to our heavenly Father. And we pray that, by his grace, we may be able to comfort others with the same comfort he has given us (2 Corinthians 1:4).

Forging Fellowship Reflections

1. If we perceive our subjective suffering as the worst, how can we get past our suffering to care for the needs of others? (Think of Jesus suffering on the cross: three of his seven last recorded words were directed at others—his mother, one of the thieves, and his persecutors.)

2. How much suffering do you think a person has to go through to be able to speak about lessons learned?

3. Did any of Paul's stories resonate with you? Which ones?

Learning to Trust Anyway

Dave and Erin's Story

Our cause is never more in danger than when a human, no longer desiring, but still intending, to do our enemy's [God's] will, looks round upon a universe from which every trace of him seems to have vanished, and asks why he has been forsaken, and still obeys.

C. S. LEWIS, UNCLE SCREWTAPE IN
THE SCREWTAPE LETTERS

Paul. When we first had the chance to engage in a deeper conversation, I could sense that there was a hardship-induced depth in your spirit that seemed greater than your chronological years. Tell us where that sense of suffering-deepened character came from?

Dave. When you asked me at Urbana 12, "What causes you to suffer?" there was primarily one area of my life that caused me great pain: my wife's degenerative eye condition. This pain continues, but since our conversation then, our suffering has expanded greatly due to the trials we experienced regarding adoption. I'll get to these later.

Paul. Certainly one of the worst forms of suffering is to see a loved one in pain and be unable to solve the issue or relieve the pain. Tell us more about Erin's eye condition.

Dave. Actually, to help explain what I might call my shared suffering with my wife, Erin, I'd love for readers to hear her tell her story of struggling with a challenging eye condition. While I share this pain with her, I believe this story is best told coming from her voice. Several years ago, in conjunction with a sermon on Psalm 90, Erin shared her testimony with our church family. This is her story.

Erin's Story

On the outside, I seem to lead a fairly normal life. I have a husband, a son, and a dog. I work at a counseling agency as a child and adolescent therapist, and serve at our home church, Grace Chapel, through our young adult ministry. I go for walks and for hikes. I spend time with friends. I like to eat out, travel, cook, and be creative.

The truth is, however, there is something not so normal about my life that dramatically shapes how I spend each day. I have a degenerative eye condition called retinitis pigmentosa (RP), and I am legally blind.

When I was thirteen years old I went into the eye doctor for a routine eye exam. Through the course of the appointment it became clear that there was something significantly wrong with my eyes. This discovery led to more testing, and I was eventually diagnosed with RP. What this means for me is that I have no peripheral vision, no downward vision, no night vision, and that my field of vision, which is limited already, is progressively shrinking. Currently there is no medical treatment or cure for RP, and God has not yet chosen to heal me. Without that medical or divine intervention the prognosis of my condition is that I will most likely have no remaining functional vision by the time I reach early middle age.

When I was first diagnosed with RP, I felt ashamed and embarrassed that I was different. This led me to lead a divided life. I was in complete denial that my vision was getting worse, and I lived as though it would never change. I had close friends I never told about my eye condition and played off my constant bumping into things as being ditzy or clumsy.

One of my favorite examples of just how divided my life had become is when, one day, I went to Dave and showed him my legs, full of bruises. I insisted that I had to go to the doctor immediately because, being my hypochondriac self, I was convinced that I had leukemia. I mean, how else could my legs possibly be so bruised?

Dave, being so sweet and so pastoral, sat me down and said, "Erin, you don't have leukemia and you don't need to go to the doctor. You're just legally blind and you bump into things a lot." Clearly, something needed to change in my heart.

Several years ago God really began to challenge me to lead a life of wholeness and to stop denying that RP was in fact a part of me and my future. Through this journey toward wholeness, I have learned a lot about God using me in my weakness. Someone from Scripture who really exemplifies this for me is the apostle Paul. In 2 Corinthians 12 Paul describes a "thorn in my flesh," which most scholars believe was physical in nature and some even suggest could have been visual impairment (see Galatians 4:15). As we know from Scripture, God did not choose to take away Paul's thorn, but instead used his ailments to bring God greater glory.

Sometimes, I worry that God won't be able to use me in a significant way because I am disabled, or that my life won't be as meaningful or as full. Ironically, when we in the church think of Paul the apostle, however, we don't think of him as a sick person. Rather, we look at him as a man who allowed God to use every aspect of his being. This is really who I long to be.

Around that same time when God began to call me to live with internal congruency, Dave and I came back from one of my annual eye exams feeling discouraged and frustrated. I continued to feel as though God was not going to be able to use me as fully as he would a sighted person, and was angry that this was going to have an impact on Dave as well.

The next morning, as Dave and I sat on our front porch drinking coffee, we asked ourselves, What do we want to be able to experience and achieve together during this time when we both have workable vision? Through this conversation, a verse from Psalm 90, which says, "Teach us to number our days, / that we might gain a heart of wisdom," really emerged as our prayer.

Allowing this verse to shape our lives has led to incredible things. We know that we have a limited number of years left where I have workable vision, and we desire to live those years with intentionality. This focus has allowed us to filter out what is important from what is trivial in life and live for things of eternal importance. Such a perspective daily prompts me to live with great conviction for causes I believe in, such as caring for and counseling at-risk children and teens.

Because I don't drive, Dave and I have chosen to live more simply and to be in a town where I experience incredible mobility through close proximity to friends, public transportation, and walking. This decision has also led us to live in closer community with our neighbors. But most important, we have grown to cherish those visual snapshots of simple moments in day-to-day life, moments such as a beautiful sunset.

My life might be different, but different isn't always bad. God calls us to faithfulness regardless of life's condition. I think that too often suffering or things not being perfect or not as we think they should be can lead us to bitterness. This is not how God wants us to respond. When we face trials and hard times, we should seek to live with intentionality through those times. I admit that I don't live every day free from the temptation to become bitter.

There are many when I become frustrated with God, but I am learning to submit my life to him and allow him to use me as he wishes. Each of us needs to be intentional, to look for what God wants to teach us and how he wants to shape us. The reality is none of us are promised that things will be the same tomorrow as they are today, and so we must live with a sense of urgency to demonstrate faithfulness in this moment.

✦ ✖ ✦

Paul.   Thanks for sharing Erin's story because it exemplifies so many of the ideas we hope to convey in this book—most notably her choice and yours to grow with intentionality in spite of the present and future challenges. Choosing how we respond to hardship usually presents us with our greatest crisis and opportunity.

Dave.   Erin's perspective, and her whole life for that matter, embodies to me how we can best go about living fully and faithfully despite the unwelcome presence of suffering in our lives. Her story has inspired and helped so many people who struggle with disabilities of many kinds—including those with legal blindness. But she's impacted no one to a greater extent than me. Learning to suffer through the emotional pain of her eye condition helped to prepare us to endure through what have since been the most devastating realities of our lives: two failed adoptions.

Paul.   What is the background of why you pursued adoption rather than starting a family in the "normal" biological way?

Dave. During our time as college students, Erin and I served at local orphanages on short-term mission trips to the Dominican Republic. For the first time in our lives, we encountered poverty like we had never seen before. Our hearts became utterly broken as we saw the plight of the orphaned and abandoned firsthand. Like many who have had experiences like these, we vowed to do something about it. We decided that instead of attempting to build our family by having children biologically, we would first begin by attempting to adopt one or more of the 130 million orphaned children in the world.[1]

Paul. Entering into the suffering of the world's orphan crisis is a worthy pursuit. But most often, it can be extremely challenging. What was this process like for you and Erin?

Dave. At first, this process proved to be exhilarating and exciting. We felt privileged to be called by God to take on a challenge this large and all-encompassing. Soon into the process, though, we realized this vow could take years to fulfill. The countries we thought we would be able to adopt from closed their doors to international adoption. We felt that excruciating frustration of wanting to help but not being able to.

Just as we were growing increasingly disheartened by the roadblocks throughout this process, we were invited by our adoption agency to join a pilot international adoption program. It seemed like after three years of getting nowhere, we were finally beginning to see an end in sight. Around that same time, another opportunity to adopt that we weren't anticipating came out of nowhere. The local branch of our agency approached us about adopting an elementary-age child who was being given up for adoption. The social workers thought we would be a great fit for this child, and so after a short but intensive time of prayer and discernment, we decided to accept this opportunity. And just like that, in a matter of a couple of days, this child was in our home and was in the process of becoming our new child. We couldn't believe it!

Like all the adoption stories we had heard, the beginning days with this first child were filled with a series of highs and lows. Within a few days, though, the lows become far lower than we could have imagined.

The trauma this child experienced prior to coming into our home was far more severe than anything we or our agency could have envisioned. Due to this, we sought additional medical and professional help. This counsel revealed that this child required intensive and specialized care that we would not be able to provide in our home. A new, temporary plan was developed that we quickly put into action. Through the paperwork we were completing for this care plan to be enacted, we learned the most disheartening news of our lives. Despite all the work we completed with our agency to adopt this child, there were unforeseen legal complications that would prevent us from being able to complete the process.

Paul. What a complicated combination of disappointments and pain: entering into the child's pain, experiencing disappointment with the legal process, and pouring your heart out only to confront loss.

Dave. Indeed, we had never felt so kicked in the gut or so disoriented ever before. One day we were experiencing the exhilaration of being called Mom and Dad for the first time, and then less than three weeks later we were told that we would be unable to adopt this child. Along with this, it was determined that it was in the child's best interest for us to not continue on in any form of supportive role. It was the saddest and most upsetting news we had ever been given. Our hearts were broken as we said the hardest goodbye of our lives—to a child who wanted to call us Mom and Dad.

Paul. How did you process this together?

Dave. Through all of our grief, all of our disappointment, all of the pain we felt for the injustices this child went through, we learned an important lesson. When you step into the brokenness of this world as a servant, you should prepare for your life and your heart and your story to be broken as well. Service leaves scars. And really, what else should we expect? This is the very result Jesus experienced as he served to make us his own.

Over the course of the next several months, we lamented like we never had before. Prayers were often at best nothing more than groans. Our bones ached. Our home felt like a constant memorial to all that was lost.

Paul. Sounds like you could have fit well into Christie's prayer chair.

Dave. Yes, but through all of this anguish, gratefully, we slowly began to recover and started to feel a greater solidarity with each other, with our church community, and especially with Christ. Our lives were being put back together by the grace of God. We *were* going to make it.

As we reflected on all the events that transpired over this season, we began to realize that we had learned so much about trauma and how to parent a child who had undergone such unfathomable realities. Experiential knowledge like this could only have come through trial. So what were we going to do with all that we'd come to learn? How might God want to use it? We began asking, What might this trial in our adoption story be preparing us for in the future?

The answer that started to emerge was that we should consider being open to children who have experienced more severe forms of trauma than we were originally open to.

About six months after this local child was in our home, we heard about a group of elementary-age half-siblings on the waiting children's list from the country we were still seeking to adopt from.

While this seemed too daunting to pursue, as we thought and prayed about it, a picture of this being able to work grew in our minds. It's been said that a vision is a picture of the future that you cannot let go of. As much as we tried to walk away from attempting to adopt these children, we couldn't. We had a vision that wouldn't let go.

Paul. So what happened next?

Dave. To ensure we didn't pursue this unwisely, we set up a list of five or six things that would have to occur for us to feel confident enough to move forward. Much to our surprise, all of the barriers we set up in order to stop this adoption journey with these kids were removed. This included receiving major financial gifts to make this situation viable and receiving affirmation from several of the leading adoption and attachment specialists in our region that this situation could work. We couldn't believe it. This was going to be the biggest act of faith in our lives, but it truly seemed like God was leading the way.

Paul.   When you say "it truly seemed like," I get concerned that this story has pain ahead.

Dave.   Indeed, but we obviously didn't know that then. One year after our attempt at local adoption, we traveled internationally to adopt this sibling group. We met the kids and their caregivers immediately upon our arrival at the airport, and we could not have been happier. It seemed like this was exactly what God had in mind for our adoption journey all along.

A few days into our trip, though, everything changed. We learned information about the children's situation that no one from our partnering adoption agencies knew anything about. It was the sort of information that would have negated this whole endeavor from ever beginning. We were left in disbelief. We had done so much work, traveled so far, made ourselves so vulnerable—again—for this to be happening. Through the counsel of the local social workers, we decided to let this situation play out and trust and believe God for a miracle. Apart from his miraculous intervention, this opportunity stood no chance at success.

Although we saw real signs of hope along the way, after about four weeks of trying to make this situation work, it became clear that the wisest and most loving thing we could do for these children was *not* to pursue adopting them any further. I wrote to our church leaders and those supporting us along the way that this was "the worst right decision" we have ever had to make. Nearly a couple years later, that description still rings true.

Paul.   I know that you encountered very deep pain in this experience. Obviously there was your pain of having to say goodbye again to children who wanted to call you Mom and Dad. But you again encountered trauma and pain in children—suffering caused by others—that left you feeling that lamentation of the brokenness in the world.

Dave. Absolutely. After the children left our care, and our through-the-roof fight-or-flight responses began to subside, we felt submerged into a drowning tide of emotions. I can vividly remember lying on the bathroom floor of the cottage where we lived with the kids feeling as if every joint in my body were pulled out of socket. There was so much emotional pain that it literally felt physical. And yet other moments we felt so stunned that we didn't feel anything at all. This absence of pain felt like the temporary shock one experiences directly after an injury has occurred before the onset of excruciating pain sets in. Except in this case, this feeling of shock wouldn't dissipate. The pain we wanted to feel to be able to grieve wouldn't come. It was as cruel as death.

Paul. You describe the pain of traumatic loss vividly. Anyone who has lost a child in any number of ways might identify with your words.

Dave. And the pain continued. In our most honest moments throughout the seemingly endless shock, neither of us really knew if we could get back up off that bathroom floor. We didn't know what would happen next. We didn't know if we could go on.

Unquestionably, this was the single most crushing and defeating experience of our lives. We felt totally humiliated to undergo such a failure yet again. We felt let down by all those we trusted with our adoption journey. Our vision to adopt seemed dashed, trampled on, ruined. How could this happen to us—twice now?

Paul.   Did any of this anger or frustration point Godward?

Dave.   Of course! And often in a pretty uncensored fashion! We were enraged that God would allow children to experience trauma so intense that it would lead to all we witnessed. Why? And most perplexing of all to us: *Why would God call us to do something that couldn't be done?*

As a pastor who loves his church, I wanted to run away from our congregation. I wanted to spare them from all this pain we would bring home. I honestly thought protecting our community from the devastation they would feel watching us go through such a heart-wrenching experience again would be the wisest way to shepherd the flock. I felt so strongly about this that I even offered to resign from my position at the church if my senior pastor thought that best for our people. Fortunately, and by God's grace, he did not think that would be a good thing for our church at all.

Paul.   I remember well our conversations shortly after this—when I was on the same continent but in a different country.

Dave.   The words of encouragement that you offered turned out to be prophetic for us. You said, "I think that leading by example to the Grace Chapel family through the disappointment and the 'we really don't understand why' times is arguably more important than the 'celebrate our successes' times. It's a Job-like 'though he slay me yet will I trust him' faith that holds us secure in the traumas of life."

Trusting those words to be true became our motivation for returning home and picking back up where we left off, disappointment, defeat, and all.

Paul.   I imagine some of our readers might be finding themselves in a place similar to this right now. Share with us one of the moments of breakthrough that you experienced that enabled you and Erin to begin recapturing hope and purpose.

Dave. One of the biggest breakthroughs for us came totally unexpectedly. Months earlier, one of my friends sent me Tim Keller's book on faith and work, *Every Good Endeavor*. I hadn't touched it since it arrived, but for some reason its red cover happened to grab my attention one day. At the time, this didn't strike me as a "take and read" moment like Saint Augustine had, but in hindsight I don't doubt at all that it was the Holy Spirit bringing this book to my attention.

In its earliest pages, Keller recounts J. R. R. Tolkien's story *Leaf by Niggle*. In this short story the artist, Niggle, is attempting to paint one last picture before the "necessary long journey" of death called him. The image was to be of a tree that opened out to a glorious country never before seen. While Niggle worked and worked on this project, the most progress he was ever able to make was the painting of just one small leaf of the tree. When death inevitably found Niggle, he lamented over just how unfinished this work of his was.

But the story of Niggle doesn't end at his death. In the afterlife, Niggle is put on a train toward the mountains of a heavenly existence. Along this journey, much to his surprise, Niggle sees the tree he struggled to paint right before him—completed in all its beauty and glory. What Niggle failed to accomplish in his lifetime was there waiting for him in the life to come.

In the same way, Keller comments how every one of us is a Niggle. We all imagine achieving things that we won't end up accomplishing in our lifetimes. Yet this life and its disappointments are not all there is. Keller writes, "If the God of the Bible exists . . . and this is not the only life, then every good endeavor, even the simplest ones, pursued in response to God's calling, can matter forever."[2] In the midst of such irresolution as ours, there was reason to hope. There was reason to keep going. Perhaps there is more to our story than we can see.

Niggle's story resounds with the heart of Paul's words in 1 Corinthians 15:58, which became my constant companion during this dark season: "be steadfast, immovable, always abounding in the work of the Lord, knowing that in the Lord your labor is not in vain" (ESV). What a promise: "your labor is not in vain." Our adoption efforts were not in vain. How could we go on? By believing our work was not in vain. How could we trust God? By remembering there really is a tree.

Paul. Even as we write this book, you've told me that you're still processing these painful experiences. Where are you and Erin now?

Dave. As we strove to trust God even when we didn't want to, we slowly began to feel like we were being lifted off that bathroom floor. Jerry Sittser's words from his book *A Grace Disguised* brought us continual inspiration: "It is not, therefore, the *experience* of loss that becomes the defining moment of our lives, for that is as inevitable as death, which is the last loss awaiting us all. It is how we *respond* to loss that matters."[3]

We are profoundly thankful that by God's work in our lives, we were able to rise with a newfound strength we never could have anticipated. So much of the healing that occurred in the aftermath of this huge disappointment came through God's gracious provision in the countless words and acts of love from our friends, family, and especially our amazing church community. So many knew exactly what it meant to be a part of this fellowship of the suffering with us. We could not have been more grateful.

When we finally felt somewhat resettled to our life, we decided to try building our family the old-fashioned way, since we were 0-2 with adoption. By the gift of God, our son, Dallas, was given to us. He was born exactly one year, and one day, after we returned from our attempt at adopting internationally.

Paul. Do we need to tell readers that he is named after one of your favorite authors, Dallas Willard, and not the city, the football team, or the old TV show?

Dave. I think you just told them! Dallas's arrival has presented us with new opportunities to process our painful adoption attempts. Many who have been confounded by what God was doing through our failed adoption efforts have tried to tell us that Dallas must have been God's plan all along. As well-meaning as we know many of these sentiments were, we hesitate to affirm them. We cannot imagine God devising a plan in which children would be treated so dismissively and recklessly.

While our son brings us great joy, we don't view him as the resolution to our past disappointments. We hold the joy we experience parenting him right alongside the pain we still feel for the children who once called us Mom and Dad. Their lives will always stay with us in our scars.

Paul. Excellent reminder that pain lives on in us. Finally, how have you found your stories woven into the greater community of the "fellowship of the suffering" that we've described?

Dave. While much of what Erin and I have experienced cannot be nicely summed up or neatly explained, we find ourselves in good company. We find ourselves not only in community with one another or even with the people throughout Scripture, but also with God himself. Eugene Peterson captures this reality powerfully:

> The biblical revelation neither explains nor eliminates suffering. It shows, rather, God entering into the life of suffering humanity, accepting and sharing the suffering. Scripture is not a lecture from God, pointing the finger at unfortunate sufferers and saying, "I told you so: here and here and here is where you went wrong; now you are paying for it." Nor is it a program from God providing, step by step, for the gradual elimination of suffering in a series of five-year plans (or, on a grander scale, dispensations). There is no progress from more to less suffering from Egyptian bondage to wilderness wandering, to kingless anarchy, to Assyrian siege, to Babylonian captivity, to Roman crucifixion, to Neronian/Domitian holocaust. The suffering is there, and where the sufferer is, God is.[4]

Our suffering in *this* world is not going to go away. But neither is our God! He is with us—no matter the pain, no matter the heartache, not even when we think he's left us. In fact, Jesus can even relate to the moments when we feel abandoned by God. On the cross, he himself cried out the agonizing words "My God, my God, why have you forsaken me?" (Matthew 27:46). Jesus paradoxically knows what it's like to feel left by God. Thus there's never an experience of suffering that we go through that Jesus cannot relate to.

Knowing this, we have found our souls strengthened, enlivened, and more hopeful than ever. To us, "the fellowship of the suffering"—with Christ and his church—has been a foretaste of "the glory about to be revealed to us" (Romans 8:18 NRSV). *Where the sufferer is, God is.*

Forging Fellowship Reflections

1. How might Dave and Erin's examples—albeit far from perfect ones—guide you to live more fully and faithfully despite your suffering?

2. When, if ever, have you sensed God leading you to do something that would eventually fail? How did you respond? How might God be inviting you to learn to trust him despite the disappointments and hardships you've encountered?

PART TWO

fellowship
with Christ

The Sun Comes from the Dark

Prayer Through Suffering

If your heart is broken, you'll find God right there;
if you're kicked in the gut, he'll help you catch your breath.

PSALM 34:18, *THE MESSAGE*

REENTERING AMERICAN LIFE after the overseas failed adoption was one of the most jostling and disorienting seasons of life that Erin and I (Dave) ever experienced. We felt like bodies devoid of souls, staggering about aimlessly, hoping something might rouse us back to life. But every pleasure we thought would bring solace only added to the pain. For starters, even our home felt anything but home. The physical space was all intact, and everything was right where it belonged, but our brokenness made it feel so foreign. We felt like exiles living under our own roof.

Seeing those we loved didn't seem to make anything better either at first. As we interacted with others, we only felt utterly exposed. It seemed as if things we didn't realize about ourselves were now on full display to everyone else. People looked at us longer, slowly studying all the nuances of our suffering faces. It was as if our bodies were typing out written words that everyone but us could read. What were we saying?

The scariest aspect of being in the company of others was that after initial moments of embrace, people unintentionally postured themselves apprehensively toward us. It seemed very much how people act at a funeral or wake when they come into close proximity to an open casket. It never feels good to know your suffering is making someone else so uncomfortable. This started to make us wonder, *Are we dying?* or *Could life ever return to what we experienced as normal?* Questions like these constantly ate away at us like scavengers on flesh.

A few days after our return, the band U2 came to Boston to play four nights of consecutive shows for their "Innocence + Experience Tour." The city was abuzz. Surprisingly, though, we couldn't have cared less, which was totally out of character for us. But our friends had different plans in mind. Much like the biblical story of how a paralyzed man's group of friends got him to Jesus by tearing a roof off a home (Mark 2), so our friends tore off the roof of our reluctance to get us to go see a band we loved. (And overcame great and expensive odds to get us tickets!)

We watched most of the show in a jetlagged daze. While all of it was extraordinary—the sounds, the lights, the performance—we found ourselves struggling to enjoy it and even to stay awake. "Why did we agree to this?" we asked each other. We thought about making an early exit multiple times, but felt bad doing so after all the trouble our friends went through to get us there. But I am so glad we stayed.

Near the very end of the show, just as we were about to leave, I heard the transcendent sounds of one of the most iconic guitar intros of our lifetime, from the song "Where the Streets Have No Name." The Edge's guitar lick delivers a kind of sonic resonance that seems capable of transporting someone not only in space but also in time. Suddenly, I found myself coming back to life for a moment. Prior to this moment I didn't want to feel pleasure or enjoyment of any sort. But now I wanted "to run," and "tear down the walls" of suffering that were holding me inside. My spirit began to be lifted as I found myself singing, and my heart started believing that somehow, some way, this disappointment would not be what defined the rest of our lives. There was more.

Then, just a few minutes later, U2 finished the concert with their trademark closing song, "40." It's a song based on Psalm 40:

> I waited patiently for the LORD;
> And He inclined to me and heard my cry.
> He brought me up out of the pit of destruction, out of the
> 　　miry clay,
> And He set my feet upon a rock making my footsteps firm.
> He put a new song in my mouth, a song of praise to
> 　　our God;
> Many will see and fear
> And will trust in the LORD. (Psalm 40:1-3 NASB)

U2's version declares:

> I will sing, sing a new song
> I will sing, sing a new song . . .
>
> How long, how long, how long
> How long to sing this song

As the members of the band—Bono and the Edge, Adam and Larry—exited the stage, and the house lights came back on, the crowd started leaving but continued singing the refrain, "How long to sing this song." And they didn't stop. Down through the lifeless, concrete-walled stairwells of Boston's TD Garden and onto the streets near Legends Way, unlikely men and women of all ages continued singing these lyrics at the top of their lungs. The whole experience had a raw, primal quality to it. It was as if everyone was letting down their guard, revealing to perfect strangers that they too suffered. If only for a moment, we had all become one vast fellowship of the suffering.

Then I started to wonder if any of these people had any idea they were singing such a biblical prayer of lament. It was powerful watching many people who probably wanted nothing to do with God suddenly cry out to him with unhindered abandon. Then it dawned on me. Did I know *I* was singing? More importantly, did I realize *I* was praying a prayer of lament?

Since the final moments of the failed adoption, I not only hadn't prayed but had built up big walls around my soul to resist any temptation to pray. I wanted absolutely nothing to do with God. It had been the longest stretch I can remember since becoming a follower of Jesus that I hadn't consciously chosen to pray. And now I caught myself praying again totally by surprise! (And I haven't stopped since.) Our friends—our fellowship of the suffering—got me through the crowd, tore the roof off, and brought me to Jesus at the U2 concert.

Praying Against Your Will

Quite often, the last thing in the world we *feel* like doing when we're suffering is praying. Prayer is hard work. It requires so much of the energy we feel we no longer have, and so much of the focus we sense we've already lost. When we feel like we're at the end of our rope, we quickly dismiss prayer as a desired coping method for our grief. At first glance prayer appears to bring so little of the instant gratification that we crave when we're hurting that we almost intuitively turn to something that we think will: TV, social media, food, alcohol, painkillers. Or worse. It doesn't take long to find out (or remember) that those methods are only Band-Aids at best—

temporarily, but far from permanently, taking away our pain. At worst, they can fuel addictive behaviors that create even more pain than the hurt they were initially enlisted to eradicate.

But can prayer really be any more effective? Although it didn't seem so at first, praying through painful experiences has taught us that God must be sought after at all costs in times of hardship. Abraham Joshua Heschel contends, "When all hopes are dashed and all conceit is shattered, man begins to miss what he has long spurned. In darkness God becomes near and clear."[1] Just as the sun always comes from the darkness of night, so God becomes near and clear when we pray through our suffering.[2] Prayer creates cracks in the cloud cover of our pain to let light in—to let God in.

Let's explore how we can grow in prayer not only in spite of challenging circumstances but because of them. Specifically, we'll examine five ways we can pray through our suffering in order to cultivate deeper fellowship with God, and as a result even closer communion with his church and world. These postures of prayer include *surrendering*, *lamenting*, *contemplating*, *interceding*, and *giving thanks*. Along the way we'll discover why some of the most intimate and essential moments of fellowship with God can only be birthed out of hardship. Perhaps we'll even come to see why Eugene Peterson so boldly contends, "Prayer is suffering's best result."[3]

Surrendering

The biggest hurdle that stands in the way of praying when we're suffering is *beginning* to pray. Prayer might appear so daunting because we have no idea what to say, whether we'll be able to say anything at all, or if something really scary might come out of our mouths. Prayer can be so easily dismissed when it should be engaged, because of the many fears it elicits in us. Maybe it's the fear of failure, that praying won't go well. Or it's the fear of being uncomfortable, that being in God's presence will make us restless and overly anxious.

For many of us, trying to pray might feel like having the hard but necessary conversation we have been putting off with someone because we know it will be so awkward or so problematic. Just as it's easier to avoid having that confrontation, it's easier to resist confronting God in prayer. Yet we must pray. We can't afford *not* to. Surrendering is the leap that enables us to overcome the obstacles to fellowship with God.

Surrendering prayer is a response we offer to God when we are given circumstances we never would have chosen on our own. Because responding to God in this way is so fundamental to living in a suffering-filled world, Jesus teaches his disciples to pray these essential words for the life of faith, "Your will be done" (Matthew 6:10). In presenting us with this prayer, Jesus is inviting us to desire and trust him more than we trust ourselves—especially when the circumstances of our lives do not seem to make sense.

Perhaps the best surrendering prayer we have found to express our trust in God despite our doubts, disappointments, and disbeliefs dates back to the seventeenth century, from the pen of French philosopher and mathematician Blaise Pascal. In many ways, it is a penetrating exposition of "your will be done." We invite you to pray it as a way of expressing trust in God through surrender.

I ask you neither for health nor for sickness, for life nor for death; but that you may dispose of my health and my sickness, my life and my death, for your glory. . . . You alone know what is expedient for me; you are the sovereign master; do with me according to your will. Give to me, or take away from me, only conform my will to yours. I know but one thing, Lord, that it is good to follow you, and bad to offend you. Apart from that, I know not what is good or bad in anything. I know not which is most profitable to me, health or sickness, wealth or poverty, nor anything else in the world. That discernment is beyond the power of men or angels, and is hidden among the secrets of your Providence, which I adore, but do not seek to fathom.[4]

Jesus' mother, Mary, offers a beautiful, faithful prayer of surrender of her own, after being given the daunting news that she would be the mother of God's Son. What an unsought, unasked-for future for a mere teenager who probably was only aspiring to "fit in" at this stage of her life. Yet Mary responds to this unchosen calling with this surrendering prayer of faith: "Here am I, the servant of the Lord; let it be with me according to your word" (Luke 1:38 NRSV). Praying such faith-filled words may be far more than you're ready for at this stage in your suffering. But perhaps assuming a simple *posture of surrender* before God—without many words, or any words at all—may be a next step you are ready to take.

Learning to Surrender

Once I (Dave) started praying again after our second failed adoption, prayer took on so many varied shapes for me. Some days, entering into prayer felt like stepping into a cage match with God that I couldn't escape. I wouldn't hold back my anger, and God wouldn't get fazed by any of my attacks. We'd just go at it like Jacob as he wrestled through the night with the mysterious figure of God until the sun broke through the darkness (Genesis 32).

Other days, prayer felt like nothing except white noise. As many times as I tried to connect with God—to sense him even the slightest bit—all I heard coming from the other end of the line was static. *Perhaps the reason all this occurred was because God isn't active in the world anymore*, I wondered. That proposition absolutely terrified me.

What ultimately helped me break through into meaningful prayer with God in the intensities of my grief was sitting for hours on end in the large beanbag couch we had purchased for the children. Sitting in this beanbag became the unlikely posture of surrender that profoundly freed me to pray. The reason we bought this behemoth of a beanbag (big enough for two people to sleep on side-by-side) was because it was good for sensory reintegration. When people experience trauma at a young age, it can disrupt the signals between the brain and the different parts of the body. Thus, one of the real injustices of trauma and abuse is that it disables many victims from being able to consistently identify reality and themselves accurately. By spending time in such an engulfing piece of furniture, our hope was that our children's abilities to properly sense their environment would be better restored. The irony of this beanbag, though, is that what we purchased to heal others became the primary means through which God restored me. By praying on this beanbag, my life became reintegrated with him.[5]

The way this happened was that I would generally set aside one large block of time each day to simply sit as motionless as possible on this beanbag as a way of positioning my life before God. Because I am naturally an energetic, wired kind of person, sitting still for extended periods of time, or even for brief stretches of time, is hard for me. But because this beanbag was so immersive, I was able to be still despite my restlessness, and as a result of my stillness, I begin to know God again (Psalm 16:11). As I sensed God surrounding me, I felt compelled to surrender to him like never before.

Tim Keller writes in his book *Prayer*, "Is it possible for a man or woman to come to love God for Himself alone, so that there is a fundamental contentment in life despite the circumstances? Yes, but only through prayer."[6] By simply sitting still and silently before God in prayer and surrendering my agenda to him, I grew convicted of the reality that I had been *loving my mission for God more than I was loving God himself.* In other words, I loved the idea of doing something great for God more than I loved my great God.

One of the hardest losses for me in these two failed adoptions was not just the loss of the presence of these children in my life (which was excruciatingly painful), but the loss of feeling called by God to do something radical. During some of the most formative years of my faith, this message seemed to be voiced over and over again: to ensure you do not waste your life, don't live an ordinary Christian life but a *radical* one. Break the norms, take risks, "expect great things from God; attempt great things for God." While there's nothing inherently wrong with these challenges, for me they became *an idol*: a good thing I made into an *ultimate* thing.

We thought starting our family through adoption instead of biologically was part of our radical calling. When this failed to work out, it unearthed a lot of the inferior "loves" that were motivating me, instead of my love for God and, even more so, God's love for me. If I'm really honest, I think taking on a big risk like this was a way for me to justify just how seriously I took the Bible and my devotion to God. It was a way for me to prove myself to others and my worth to God. I wasn't just going to follow the pattern of what most other Christians did. I was going to do something great for God—as if living an ordinary, faithful, and good life for him wasn't great. (Something I've come to respect now more than ever.)

Through *surrendering* prayer, I had to ask, *What was motivating me to strive to do something radical?* Perhaps something I hadn't been aware of before. The answer: my own insecurities. I had (and still do at times) a real need to stand out from my peers—whether they be other pastors or other Christians around my age. As I sat on this beanbag, available before God and vulnerable before him—surrendering moment by moment—this realization finally came to light in my soul. The contentment I was after, even before these adoption efforts, could never be met by accomplishing something great for God, but only in relishing Christ's great accomplishment for me. Wanting God for his sake became my new motivation moving forward, and over time it brought with it a contentment I never knew I could experience. Through the humiliation of these experiences, I came to understand far more fully what Tim Keller meant when he said, "You don't really know Jesus is all you need until Jesus is all you have."[7]

While I never would have chosen these trials, I never could have received so much insight and so much communion with God apart from them. Through all of my pain, God has become nearer and clearer to me than ever before. His kingdom has advanced in my heart like I never could have anticipated. Suffering has resulted in teaching me that prayer is primarily about being with God to love him, more than it is about recruiting God to help me do all that I want to accomplish for him.

We are convinced, though, that the enemy is doing everything in his power to prevent us from praying like this. Even though prayer feels unwanted at times when we're hurting, it is the way to what we need most: fellowship with God. Surrender enables us to break through the barriers to communion with him in prayer. We can surrender by simply showing up, being still, and waiting on God. Agenda free. Again and again. Over and over. Through this repeated surrender, trust is born. In trusting God, we're given the eyes of faith to believe that he not only hears our cries but answers our prayers. As Keller wisely concludes, "God answers all our prayers. He gives us what we want or what we would have asked for if we knew everything he knew."[8] Could it be possible that if you knew all that God knows, you would have asked God for what you're experiencing now?

No matter what you're facing today, know that God ultimately *knows*, and he can be trusted. Never stop surrendering to him.

Lamenting

No form of prayer is perhaps harder for good Christian people than lamenting. In many of our households growing up, we were taught to always be polite. We were instructed to not raise our voices. We were commanded that "if you can't say anything nice, you shouldn't say anything at all." Expressing anger, frustration, and injustice has no fitting place for "nice" people. Not only that, but many of us were told it was a sign of weakness to show any signs of grief. "Crying is for babies." "Suck it up." We were implicitly promised that if we kept our pain to ourselves, it would simply go away.

But there's nothing biblical about any of these traditions passed down to us. The witness of the Bible is that fellowship with God is filled repeatedly with lament. Approximately two-thirds of the psalms are prayers of lament: cries, groans, rages of anger, passionate pleas for justice, denunciations of enemies. Nothing appears off-limits. Only, perhaps, inauthentic, "nice" and polite prayers. God never calls his people to pretend. Listen to some examples:

> How long, LORD? Will you forget me forever?
>   How long will you hide your face from me?
> How long must I wrestle with my thoughts
>   and day after day have sorrow in my heart?
>   How long will my enemy triumph over me?
>   (Psalm 13:1-2)

Why, O LORD, do you reject me
and hide your face from me?
From my youth I have been afflicted and close to death;
I have suffered your terrors and am in despair. . . .
You have taken my companions and loved ones from me;
the darkness is my closest friend. (Psalm 88:14-15, 18
NIV 1984)

Tucked away in the Old Testament is an entire book dedicated to voicing the deepest angst of ravaged people: Lamentations. Why is an entire book dedicated to such an uncomfortable, off-limits kind of topic? Because through the honest expressions of our suffering, we forge fellowship with our God who is a fellow sufferer.

The very structure of Lamentations provides a fascinating lesson that can teach us how to pray through our suffering. Eugene Peterson observes that the laments found in the book are composed on an alphabetic structure as acrostics. (An acrostic is a poetic form of writing in which each line of the poem begins with its corresponding letter in the [Hebrew] alphabet.) What is so surprising about this is that while the acrostic form of writing is highly structured, prayers birthed out of suffering are most often wildly spontaneous, erratically emotive even. Why then would the form of an acrostic be appropriate to express the anguish of lament? Peterson's contention is that the acrostic is used "to guarantee that the grief and despair are expressed completely. The acrostic patiently, and carefully, goes through the letters of the alphabet and covers the ground of suffering. Every detail of suffering comes under consideration."[9] Lamentations 2:18 is a prime example of how the Scriptures instruct us not to hurry as we lament over our hurts:

Cry out to the Lord . . .
let your tears flow like a river

day and night;

give yourself no relief,

your eyes no rest.

There's a remarkable brilliance to this, because as people, most of our natural instincts tell us to get through our times of grieving as quickly as possible. Given this human tendency, this structure of prayer offers a most helpful corrective. It teaches us that we should not hurry as we walk with grief, that we should not try to get through to the other side of it as quickly as possible. Rather, we should patiently and courageously wade through all the variant waters of our suffering so that we might most fully encounter God. We need not fear holding back, either. Or of drowning. For Jesus is "a man of suffering, and familiar with pain" in all its pervasive nature (Isaiah 53:3). Nothing we say surprises him or catches him off guard. He is with us.

Over what areas of your life might you need to patiently lament? With what parts of your past might you need to be still before God? Whose sorrows might you need to lament for? What wrongs in our world do we need to cry out for God to make right? As we slowly and patiently present our prayers of lament to God, remember this wise instruction: "Do not hurry as you walk with grief. It does not help the journey."[10]

Contemplating

Contemplative prayer or imaginative prayer, as it can also be called, was popularized by St. Ignatius through his highly influential work *The Spiritual Exercises*. To pray contemplatively in this Jesuit tradition, a person enters into prayer by imagining a scene from Scripture through the use of all five senses to "compose the place" and setting.[11] Learning this form of prayer will be particularly helpful in forging solidarity with Christ in his sufferings and in ours. We will first introduce and practice this form of prayer, and then help you personalize it, so we may each begin to meet Jesus in our own suffering.

To begin, take a moment to read the account of Jesus praying in the Garden of Gethsemane from Matthew 26:36-46:

> Then Jesus went with his disciples to a place called Gethsemane, and he said to them, "Sit here while I go over there and pray." He took Peter and the two sons of Zebedee along with him, and he began to be sorrowful and troubled. Then he said to them, "My soul is overwhelmed with sorrow to the point of death. Stay here and keep watch with me."
>
> Going a little farther, he fell with his face to the ground and prayed, "My Father, if it is possible, may this cup be taken from me. Yet not as I will, but as you will."
>
> Then he returned to his disciples and found them sleeping. "Couldn't you men keep watch with me for one hour?" he asked Peter. "Watch and pray so that you will not fall into temptation. The spirit is willing, but the flesh is weak."
>
> He went away a second time and prayed, "My Father, if it is not possible for this cup to be taken away unless I drink it, may your will be done."
>
> When he came back, he again found them sleeping, because their eyes were heavy. So he left them and went away once more and prayed the third time, saying the same thing.
>
> Then he returned to the disciples and said to them, "Are you still sleeping and resting? Look, the hour has come, and the Son of Man is delivered into the hands of sinners. Rise! Let us go! Here comes my betrayer!"

Now that you have read through this moment in Jesus' suffering, as best as you can, try to imagine *what it might have been like* more fully by using your five senses. First, *what do you see?* What is this garden like? How many olive trees surrounded Jesus? Picture where and how he might have fallen on his face to pray in the garden. Second, *what do you hear?* Is it completely quiet, or is there noise in the background from the nearby village? Can you hear Jesus' voice as he prays? If so, what might his voice sound like? Third, *what do you feel?* Does the air feel cool or warm? What does the ground underneath your feet feel like? How do you feel internally in this tension-filled moment? Are knots in your stomach gnawing at you? Or like the disciples, are you fighting off sorrow-induced sleep? Last, *what do you smell*, and if anything, *what do you taste?* Perhaps you can smell the fragrance of the plants of the garden or taste the salt in the sweat pouring off your forehead and trickling onto your lips.

Now that you have composed a more concrete picture of this point in Jesus' life, try to get a fuller sense of the suffering he experienced in that moment. What is it like to see Jesus sorrowful to the point of death? Do you feel led to try to comfort Jesus?

This exercise of prayer could be continued by imagining ourselves as one of Jesus' disciples and experiencing this moment from one of their perspectives, or even from the perspective of Jesus himself. Hopefully, we will become more intimately familiar with the experiences of our suffering Savior through this form of prayer. Experiencing fellowship with Christ like this can breathe new life into our beaten-down souls by reminding us that Christ is not only with us but is completely familiar with all that we are going through. Contemplating other scenes of Christ's excruciating suffering can further deepen our solidarity with him. Take a few moments to remind yourself of these pain-filled points in Jesus' life:

■ Remember how Judas betrayed him.

■ Remember how Peter denied him.

■ Remember how his disciples forsook him and fled.

■ Remember his whipping.

■ Remember his crown of thorns.

■ Remember his pierced hands and feet.

■ Remember his wounded side.

■ Remember his thirst.

■ Remember his prayer of lament, "My God, my God, why have you forsaken me?"

■ Remember his death on the cross.[12]

To strengthen our fellowship with Christ continually, the scenes and events of the Passion Week should be regularly contemplated in our hearts and minds. It is particularly wise to do this when we aren't experiencing acute forms of suffering, so that when we inevitably do, we will be able to sense Jesus' presence alongside us more readily. In addition to praying through Jesus' suffering, we can also contemplate Jesus' response to the many suffering people he encounters throughout the Gospels. Whose experience of suffering in the Gospels might you identify with?

■ Jairus, who just lost his daughter (Mark 5)

■ the woman subject to twelve years of bleeding (Mark 5)

■ the man with a shriveled hand (Mark 3)

■ the woman caught in adultery (John 8)

■ Jesus as he is misunderstood by his family (Matthew 12)

As we imagine Jesus extending compassion, healing, and hope to all who are weary, we can better experience Jesus doing the same for us. Earlier we asked you to consider what causes you to suffer. Whatever it is that you *have but don't want* or *want but don't have*, picture Jesus meeting you and coming alongside you at this point of need. What is his countenance toward you? If he speaks any words, what might he say? As you meet him, ask him to give you the rest and wholeness he offers to all who are suffering and burdened (Matthew 11:28-30). Finally, receive the rest Christ extends to you, even if the source of your suffering is not taken away.

Interceding

The more fully we learn to share our suffering with God, the more capable we will become in sharing the suffering of others. Often finding a clear-cut way of bearing the burdens of others ourselves can be elusive. How do I minister to someone with a disease I can do nothing about? How can I genuinely care for someone who lives far outside of my geographic proximity? What can I really do to alleviate all the suffering that exists so pervasively and comprehensively in the world?

We start by doing what we know we can do. We can start by praying for one another. The power of intercessory prayer must never be underestimated. God uses it mightily to relieve the suffering of the world and to cultivate unbreakable Christian fellowship.

In his classic book on Christian community, *Life Together*, Dietrich Bonhoeffer writes,

> A Christian fellowship lives and exists by the intercession of its members for one another, or it collapses. I can no longer condemn or hate a brother for whom I pray, no matter how much trouble he causes me. His face, that hitherto may have been strange and intolerable to me, is transformed in intercession into the countenance of a brother for whom Christ

died, the face of a forgiven sinner. This is a happy discovery for the Christian who begins to pray for others. There is no dislike, no personal tension, no estrangement that cannot be overcome by intercession as far as our side of it is concerned. Intercessory prayer is the purifying bath into which the individual and fellowship must enter every day. The struggle we must undergo with our brother in intercession may be a hard one, but that struggle has the promise that it will gain its goal.[13]

It is all too common for fellowship in the local church to be jeopardized by any number of issues that can tear believers apart. One of the strongest defense strategies we have against this work of the devil—and our own sin!—is to pray diligently for those we have conflict with. Intercession is a critical ingredient to the lifeblood of the body of Christ. With it, we grow stronger together, as we see in each other the very face of Jesus. Just as Christ is our great High Priest, interceding for us before the Father, so we must intercede on behalf of one another. That's what a fellowship does.

Suffering can provoke intercession for others in another way. We can allow God to take our pain and use it so that we can better empathize with others. A pastor in Boston surprised his congregation when he told them that if he had a serious prayer concern, he wouldn't share it with his friends; he wasn't sure they would actually pray. Instead, he explained, he would share it with the people in church he knew were suffering from various terminal diseases like cancer. Why? "Because I know that these people are praying all the time." Those who suffer well are those who intercede.

Praying for the Persecuted Church

In our excessively practical, hands-on emphasis in ministry in Western culture, we often forget the fact that, in the words of E. M.

Bounds, "Prayer IS the ministry." We pray before ministry, as we plan for ministry, and for results in ministry, but we seldom pray as if prayer *is* the ministry.

And yet realistically—especially as we look at global ministry or ministry in cultures that neither our churches nor we will ever cross—prayer *is* our primary ministry. Paul the apostle knew that as he wrote to the Romans. He probably guessed that few of them would ever undertake the risks and ministry that occupied him daily, yet he urged them to "join me in my struggle by praying to God for me" (Romans 15:30). Again to the Corinthian believers he wrote, "[God] has delivered us from such a deadly peril, and he will deliver us again. On him we have set our hope that he will continue to deliver us, *as you help us by your prayers*" (2 Corinthians 1:10-11, italics added).

The writer of the book of Hebrews takes it a step further. He urges us to "remember those in prison [or those who are politically or socially oppressed, persecuted, beaten, even killed for their faith] as if you were together with them in prison" (Hebrews 13:3). He challenges us to empathize with these brothers and sisters.

Leaders of the International Day of Prayer for the Persecuted Church (idop.org) estimate that 150,000 Christians are killed every year for their faith, two million are persecuted (active oppression, not someone snickering in the restaurant when you bow to return thanks), and millions more live where freedom to worship and evangelize is restricted or repressed. (The annual prayer day for the persecuted church is cited on their website.)

Why not consider mobilizing your congregation in empathetic prayer for these maligned brothers and sisters this year? Praying empathetically stretches our vision and our sense of God's global purposes as it takes us places we otherwise might never go—like China, Sudan, Iran, India, and Indonesia.

After attending a quiet gathering of young Christians in a country where Christianity is severely oppressed, one of the conference leaders appealed to those of us who were flying back to the United States: "Please—don't forget us." He was asking us to join in their struggle, to help them by our prayers, to empathize with their plight as we brought them before God.[14]

Can we echo our brother's request? Please, let's not forget these people. Let's allow God to turn our pain and suffering into an opportunity to intercede for others in pain.

At the Lausanne Movement's Younger Leaders Gathering in Jakarta, Indonesia, in August 2016, one of the evening sessions focused on prayer for the persecuted church. Participants heard testimonies from a young woman who endured solitary confinement in Iran, from pastors who had suffered various persecutions in China, from a young man raised to be a jihadi in a Muslim family in Niger, from a North Korean believer, and more. For many of us living in more peaceful contexts, our personal perceived hardships seemed minimal by comparison. We prayed and worshiped and cried together with and for our suffering family.

At the close of the evening, a young Asian woman—whose own family knew persecution firsthand—led us in prayer. We include it here to inspire our own intercessory prayers for brothers and sisters all over the world:

Dear Father God, dear Lord Jesus, dear Holy Spirit,

We thank you for the peace that surpasses all our understanding. It is the peace from the cross, on which Jesus had accomplished for us all. We thank you for the models that are given to us from our seniors and our peers who have stood firm to proclaim the Jesus on the cross in the midst of persecution. We praise you that your Light shines even brighter and the joy is even bigger in the deep, deep darkness.

We pray for our dear brothers and sisters around the globe who are now suffering for the name of Jesus, including many of us who are here tonight. We claim that no suppression from the authority, no adversity from other religions, no terrorist threat could separate us from the love of Jesus, or the body of Christ. We ask for your true freedom, your true comfort and your true peace and joy to be with those who are restricted by human powers. Remember your children and fight for them and for your glory. And save the crowns of righteousness for them.

Lord, we also pray for ourselves as we bear the torch from the hands of those who gave their lives proclaiming Jesus. Let us inherit the same spirit, the spirit that inspired them and sustained them. Let us keep the memory of suffering fresh so that we can encourage those who are in sufferings. Give us strength and courage to humbly and willingly walk on the same path of Calvary that our fathers, grandfathers and saints of history have walked on.

Lord, beyond all these, we pray that you keep shaping us to be like Jesus, to live out an incarnational and sacrificial life so that the world will witness the transformational power of the cross.

We thank you for the stories that are told tonight. These are the stories that are completely different from what the world is telling. Bless us with the one same story that the power of the gospel comes from the lowest, the most humiliating place on the cross. Bless us with this power to proclaim the life of Jesus to the nations.

In the powerful name of Jesus Christ, Amen.

Giving Thanks

Finally, we can effectively pray through our suffering by continuing to give thanks. First Thessalonians 5:16-18 tells us, "Rejoice always, pray continually, give thanks in all circumstances, for this is God's will for you in Christ Jesus." God's will for us is not that we give thanks *for* our suffering, but that we continue to give thanks even in its midst.

There will rarely, if ever, be a time in our lives when it feels as if there's nothing wrong. If we all wait until times seem pain-free and problem-free to give thanks, there might never be any thanksgiving expressed. Yet without gratitude we will never taste abundance. Without gratitude our lives will be diminished. Without gratitude we will sacrifice the blessings God desires to give us.

As I (Dave) and my wife were reflecting on all the blessings God has brought into our lives, Erin said something I won't soon forget: "I feel incredibly grateful right now. But I would never have known genuine gratitude had I also not known profound grief." Somehow, paradoxically, our gratitude can enable us to get through our grief, and our grief can conversely heighten our sense of gratitude. Our suffering might always be with us in this life, but when we offer it to God and continue to give thanks even in its midst, God redeems our grief to make room for even more gratitude.

Perhaps the most beautiful example the Scriptures provide for giving thanks in the midst of suffering is the Last Supper. As the disciples join with Jesus on the eve of his crucifixion, Jesus begins their communion meal by giving thanks. Communion with God often begins with gratitude. "Give thanks *in all* circumstances." The road marked with suffering that has been laid out for us is no exception. For it's on this road that we best remember all that Jesus has done for us. He carried the heaviest burden, he hung on the loneliest cross, he entered the darkest tomb—all because of his great love for us. Because of Jesus, we have every reason to give thanks always, everywhere, without exception.

We encourage you to pause for a moment and do the hard, patient work of looking closely at your life, at God's work within and around you, and give him thanks. And then do this tomorrow, and again and again and again.

Conclusion

Prayer might be the last thing we feel like doing when we're suffering, but it's arguably the most important. Praying through suffering—our own and that of the world—brings us into closer communion not only with God but with his people throughout the world. Only through cultivating a persistent life of prayer—especially in the midst of suffering—will we be able hear Jesus' call to join him in overcoming the suffering caused by evil with his great love.

Suffering comes with the territory of following Christ because prayer is suffering's best result.

So how can we live as fully and faithfully as possible despite the unwelcome presence of suffering in our lives? We can begin by praying. To get over the hurdles that keep us from praying during times of intense suffering, perhaps you can join with Bono and the Edge, Adam and Larry, myself (Dave) and the millions of others who have sung these prayer-filled lyrics together:

How long, how long, how long
How long to sing this song?

Forging Fellowship Reflections

1. This chapter offers a list describing the progression or processing of suffering that can lead to deeper prayer: surrender, lamentation, contemplation, intercession, and giving thanks.

Which form of prayer do you think could be most helpful in this season of your life? Which of these do you find most difficult?

2. Share ideas with your fellowship small group on how we can be engaged in lamentation without getting stuck there.

Becoming the Kind of People the World Needs

Transformation Through Suffering

The "good life," comfort, convenience and a painless life have become necessities that people view as basic rights. If they do not have these, they think something has gone wrong. So when something like inconvenience or pain comes, they do all they can to avoid or lessen it. One of the results of this attitude is a severe restriction of spiritual growth, for God intends us to grow through trials.

AJITH FERNANDO, *THE CALL TO JOY AND PAIN*

BY AGE THIRTY-FIVE, given all of the accidents, stitches, surgeries, and broken bones of my adolescent years, I (Paul) thought that I had fulfilled my suffering quota for life. At age thirty-six, I ruptured my Achilles tendon playing basketball, resulting in surgery and six months of casts, crutches, therapy, and recovery, but I weathered that whole ordeal pretty well—more as an inconvenience than as suffering per se. The diagnosis of Type 1 (insulin-dependent) diabetes at age forty came as a complete lifestyle shock, but with Christie's help, we pushed through all of the adaptations and adjustments pretty well.

However, the ruptured disk two years later broke my spirit. Sciatic, burning pain in my right leg twenty-four hours a day, seven days a week: the inability to sit, stand, or even sleep comfortably. I think the writer of Psalm 38 understood: "My back is filled with searing pain; / there is no health in my body" (Psalm 38:7). Exercises didn't help. Stretching only exaggerated the pain. And pain medication was only marginally effective. The pain preoccupied all of my daily activities.

With all of the previous physical maladies I had experienced, I knew intellectually that God often used pain to develop and deepen character. I had already memorized many of the verses we cite throughout this book. But this back pain was too much.

I prayed, "Lord, if you are using this pain to refine my character and make me into a deeper man, then I ask *for shallowness*. I don't want to be a deep man that badly. Please relieve the pain."

We all might understand that God stretches us through the tough times, but none of us really want it. And thank God we are not alone. Even Jesus, when facing the cross and the fulfillment of his purpose for coming to earth, asked God to deliver him from the suffering he was about to face (Luke 22:42).

But as we understand the reality of Christian growth, or what the Bible calls being made into the image of Christ, we need to remember (in the words of Eugene Peterson), it comes with the territory. Hebrews 5:8 says that Jesus, the perfect Son of God, learned obedience through the things that he suffered. If suffering was indispensable to how Jesus Christ grew up in the faith, how much more will it be necessary for our spiritual formation?

As we experience the wilderness seasons of life, we learn that the wilderness is a place of empowerment. It shores up our weaknesses, removes our false attachments, and strengthens our capacity to know God and love the world. But the choice to grow through it is indeed a challenge.

Fostering Christian Depth

There's a story told (probably fictional or at least a little exaggerated) about a group of representatives of Christian foundations who had come together to listen to a global missions expert tell them about the state of the church around the world. The intent of the meeting was to help the foundations' representatives determine the best places to invest their funds in an effort to promote the qualitative and quantitative growth of the church around the world.

A foundation representative asked the global expert, "Given that the church in many places is described as 'miles wide and inches deep,' can you tell us the number-one factor that enhances or stimulates the church's ability to go deeper in Christlike character and discipleship?"

Without hesitation, the expert answered, "Persecution and suffering."

The foundations' representatives, knowing that persecution and suffering were not things they could or would help fund, stared at the floor for a few moments. Then another man asked, "What do you think is the *second* most significant factor?"

The lesson these funders were learning about the church at large translates down to our individual lives. Over the years we've asked dozens of older Christians the secret to growing deeper in character or Christlikeness. Inevitably the answers have come around to something related to hardship:

- Turn your hardships into greater opportunities to trust God.

- Grow through your pain.

- Character will be forged in the crucible of suffering.

- Get back up again after life has knocked you down.

- Allow the refiner's fire to burn away the imperfections.

Their words might sound harsh, but they are merely echoing the progression of Christian growth Paul cites in Romans 5:1-5:

Therefore, since we have been justified through faith, we have peace with God through our Lord Jesus Christ, through whom we have gained access by faith into this grace in which we now stand. And we boast in the hope of the glory of God. Not only so, but we also glory in our sufferings, because we know that suffering produces perseverance; perseverance, character; and character, hope. And hope does not put us to shame, because God's love has been poured out into our hearts through the Holy Spirit, who has been given to us.

Justification by faith grounds our salvation and subsequent peace with God. Through Jesus we have full access to God, which fills us with hope. As we grow, suffering comes, but we can glory in these sufferings because suffering causes us to persevere, which in turn deepens our character, which in turn fuels our hope—because our growth, as tough as it is, flows from God's love for us.

A Recurring Biblical Message

Philip Yancey (one of the most prolific Christian writers on this subject of suffering) has joined with Dr. Paul Brand in writing several books. Dr. Brand served as a medical doctor dedicated to the treatment of Hansen's disease (which we formerly called leprosy). The title of one of the books speaks to the theme of this chapter: *Pain: The Gift Nobody Wants.* The cover also includes, "Warning: Life Without Pain Could Really Hurt You," which builds off of Dr. Brand's experience working with the nerve-numbing desensitization to pain, the early symptoms of leprosy.

Dear Lord, No Suffering for Me Please

Dear Lord,

I have a somewhat strange proposal. But I think that when considered, you will find my rationality very reasonable. Lord, I know that we as Christians must share in the sufferings of Christ. I know that one of the unavoidable things about life is suffering. I also know that although you may not actually cause the suffering, you use it for the benefit of your kingdom. Natural disasters, broken relationships, persecution, financial and professional struggles as well as sickness and death will come.

But, Lord, could you make my life an exception? I'd really prefer if I didn't have to suffer all that much. A more peaceful, hassle-free life without too many struggles would be nice. My proposal is as follows: If I find other ways to sanctify myself, could you perhaps allow me to miss the pain and suffering part of life?

I'd like to summarize, at the risk of being wrong, what I know are some causes for suffering and show you how I could be sanctified by alternate means. The first reason I know is that we live in a fallen world and sin reigns in the hearts of men. That is, we suffer because we or others have been selfish and sinful. Although I cannot take responsible for others, I can take responsibility for myself. With your help Lord, like Job I can consciously commit to flee from the indulgences of sex, money, and power that encroach on your good will. That would just leave the sin of others to worry about. To compensate for their sinfulness I could volunteer with the oppressed, impoverished, and downtrodden. That way I would see the plight of wickedness and fight it tooth and nail without experiencing it myself.

Secondly, suffering could also come as some type of trial, test, or discipline. We could suffer because you test our heart to see if it matches our words. I wish to also use others as a way out of such suffering. I could counsel on a regular basis those who are being tested and sympathize, empathize, and pray for them. I could then take their difficulties and ask my wife to test me at an unknown time whether I really trust you. For example, to see whether I trust you for food she could covertly remove anything with sustenance from our house to see how I respond. She could even temporarily give me only an unworkable sum of money every day and test my reaction. This way any suffering could be minimal and effective at the same time.

We could also possibly suffer because of righteousness. This, I believe, is when the goodness of Christ comes in conflict with the sinfulness of the world. Like Jesus being called a demon because he was performing miracles. From the beatitudes we know that those who suffer for righteousness will behold the kingdom of heaven. This is a tricky one and I am starting to think I may have to suffer a little. But I must admit, Lord, that I think righteousness has actually benefited me more than it has allowed me to suffer. For example, the other day a police officer came to my house to verify my address in order for me to procure my passport. He asked for a bribe and I gave him a lecture on integrity instead. He seemed ashamed and left after listening to and accepting my rebuke. I would have suffered if he had declined me a passport but I got my passport soon after. So Christ's righteousness in this case allowed me to challenge a cop for doing wrong while acquiring a passport at the same time. If all my good acts could reap such double-benefits, Lord, that would be nice.

Lastly, there are reasons for suffering that we cannot possibly know or understand. This reasoning is the trickiest because I cannot know how you are working through the suffering and therefore cannot preempt a proper response. It is interesting to note here how you did not actually give Job an answer to his question "Why?" You did ask him a lot of questions about nature in response though. You said things like "Who has let the wild donkey go free?" and "The wings of the ostrich wave proudly but are they the pinions and plumage of love?" I think I know what you are getting at. You wanted him to endure and trust and know that you are sovereign. He probably never knew in his lifetime that his story would become an example for solace to millions of suffering people. But he did seem to realize, through your nature questions, that your wisdom and care is far beyond our own.

To learn the lesson of suffering we cannot understand, I will not seek to understand anything; I will simply look to nature and bathe in its wonder and awe. I can spend regular retreats in the wild, searching out things that are too wonderful for me. I'll study the ants, the ostriches, and the mountain goats and gaze at the beauty of life. I must admit, Lord, I did have such an experience of awe recently when my daughter was born. The moment she came out I had a deep sense of beauty and wonder where I simultaneously wanted to shrivel up in amazement and shout out in joy. Nature will humble me into realizing that there are many things that are too wonderful to fathom. I'll understand that "why?" is not the right question, and dwell on "wow" as the answer.

So, I think I have covered all my bases, Lord. I'll learn my all my lessons in a controlled environment where I don't have to suffer and life will be a breeze. I think you'll find my reasoning quite good. What I am really asking, Lord, is if I can suffer just a little less? Of course, I have nothing to offer you in return. Only that I will try and learn the right lessons. Strangely, I am now realizing that my argument does not seem very persuading.

Ok, God, how about I suffer but only over a short period of time? If it could all be within a short stretch then the rest of my life could be hassle-free. If the suffering was condensed and I knew it was for a short time that

would not be as bad. I have just realized that in the scale of eternity our life is a very short time, so that argument may backfire on itself. But what I mean is that there is so much to enjoy on this earth and it would be a shame if so much of life was spent in misery.

Lord, I know my requests might seem a little strange, but, since I am asking, would it be possible if you could keep my family from suffering also? Also, if you could keep my immediate family from pain that would be nice. Why not throw in my extended family too? I believe some of my friends would thrive in a suffering-free environment, but I'll let that be up to your discretion. Just one more request, Lord: if you could reply to this letter with either a very deep, audible voice, or by turning the clouds into letters, those would be the best communication methods.

Yours gratefully,

Jonathan Abraham

Using his patients as an example, Dr. Brand shows that their responses to the pain and the choices that they make when confronted with the disease often determine their long-term prognosis. He parallels this in all of our lives as we face pain:

> Each of these groups of people [his patients in various locales] helped to form my outlook on this mysterious fact of human existence. Most of us will one day face severe pain. I am convinced that the attitude we cultivate in advance may well determine how suffering will affect us when it does strike.[1]

The Bible echoes this same theme: What will we do in the face of pain, suffering, hurt, even persecution? The first and most basic response is to ask God to take it away. If Jesus asked God to remove the suffering ahead of him, it's okay for us to ask the same.

The bigger issue occurs when God doesn't answer our request—or at least he doesn't answer as we might like. Then we will find ourselves challenged either to invite God to use pain to help us grow or to run away in pursuit of shallowness. We will find ourselves challenged by in the words of the Serenity Prayer used by Alcoholics Anonymous: will we accept "hardships as the pathway to peace"?

Consider the humorous prayer in the sidebar offered by our Indian colleague Jonathan Abraham as he voices the feelings that many of us have regarding suffering and transformation.

The Bible provides us with multiple examples where growth and suffering—combined with our human response—work together:

- After incredible physical suffering combined with personal loss of loved ones, Job concludes that suffering had brought him to a new depth of relationship with God: "My ears had heard of you / but now [after all I've been through], my eyes have seen you" (Job 42:5).

▨ The psalmist exhorts patience in the face of hardship:

> *I would have despaired* unless I had believed that I would
> see the goodness of the LORD
> In the land of the living.
> Wait for the LORD;
> Be strong and let your heart take courage;
> Yes, wait for the Lord. (Psalm 27:13-14 NASB)

▨ David observes that suffering provoked great obedience. "Before I was afflicted I went astray, / but now I obey your word (Psalm 119:67).

▨ He reiterates the same message, citing the positive impact in his life: "It was good for me to be afflicted / so that I might learn your decrees" (Psalm 119:71).

▨ Jeremiah voices his complaint before God concerning his physical, relational, emotional, and spiritual suffering. But then he focuses on God's faithfulness and steadfast love. He concludes,

> The LORD is good to those whose hope is in him,
> to the one who seeks him;
> it is good to wait quietly
> for the salvation of the LORD.
> It is good for a man to bear the yoke
> while he is young.
> Let him sit alone in silence,
> for the LORD has laid it on him. (Lamentations 3:25-28)

▨ The early church understood that hardship came with the decision to follow Jesus: "We must go through many hardships to enter the kingdom of God" (Acts 14:22).

▨ Paul exhorted the Corinthian believers not to lose heart in the face of hardship "for our light and momentary troubles are achieving for us an eternal glory that far outweighs them all" (2 Corinthians 4:17).

■ The writer of Hebrews, writing to encourage Christians not to quit the faith in the face of opposition and persecution, reminded them of the refining power of suffering toward holiness, righteousness, and peace. "Endure hardship as discipline; God is treating you as his children. . . . God disciplines us for our good, in order that we may share in his holiness. No discipline seems pleasant at the time, but painful. Later on, however, it produces a harvest of righteousness and peace for those who have been trained by it" (Hebrews 12:7, 10-11).

■ Peter, writing to the same type of struggling first-century Christians, reminded them that "Since Jesus went through everything you're going through and more, learn to think like him. Think of your sufferings as a weaning from that old sinful habit of always expecting to get your own way. Then you'll be able to live out your days free to pursue what God wants instead of being tyrannized by what you want" (1 Peter 4:1-2 *The Message*).

■ James identifies an even more distinctive purpose in our sufferings—trials build patience. "Consider it pure joy, my brothers and sisters, whenever you face trials of many kinds, because you know that the testing of your faith produces perseverance. Let perseverance finish its work so that you may be mature and complete, not lacking anything" (James 1:2-4).

The Big Question: How Big Is Our God?

Everyone wants a God who they can simultaneously worship, understand, and, if we'd admit it, control. We want a God who loves us, wants our best, and grants our requests. The musical group

Jethro Tull illustrated this years ago when they inverted the words of Genesis and observed, "In the beginning, man made God in his own image." Humankind needed an object of worship, so they made an "enlarged human." Others describe our desire for a powerful God who is predictable and gives us just want we want as we ask—a "celestial Santa," if you will.

But life and spirituality don't work out that way. At times, we bow at the realization of God's awesomeness, but he doesn't act in the predictable way we desire. To borrow from C. S. Lewis's The Chronicles of Narnia, God is good, but he's not safe.

Sometimes we get the answers to prayer that we desire, but then we wonder why God doesn't act in power to stop the things we know are wrong. Or why he heals one person and allows another to die. Or why a child is killed in a car accident. Or why does God allow a godly parent to wither away for a decade with Alzheimer's?

Suffering, hardship, and unanswered prayer cause us to face some choices in the way we understand God.

- Will we choose a syrupy religion and a sugary view of life, where spirituality means trying to sugarcoat all of life's harsh realities—even to the point where we become those offering a defense for God?

- Or we will come to a cynical withdrawal from God—concluding, based on our experiences and the experiences of others, that either God does not exist (atheism) or he exists but simply does not care or does not involve himself in the affairs of humankind (deism)?

- Or will we choose to believe either that although God hates evil and suffering, he is powerless to prevent it and answer prayer (as Rabbi Harold Kushner chooses in *Why Bad Things Happen to Good People*) or that God is capricious, unknowable, and unpredictable, randomly bringing good to some and evil on others (as in some forms of fatalistic Islam)?

Thinking Biblically

The biblical presentation of God is a bigger and less cut-and-dried view of God than we might expect or desire. On the one hand, God is presented as sovereign and apparently working bigger purposes that transcend our understanding. On the other hand, God hears our prayers, comforts us in our afflictions, and—in the person of Jesus Christ—suffers with us and for us (Philippians 2:5-11).

Let's look to the Scriptures with a few questions—so that we can evaluate our view of God against the biblical presentation. As we face the reality of life's hardships, suffering, pain, and prison, our basic question is this: *Is our God simultaneously big enough and close enough?*

Is our God big enough to make the rules? We all want a little bit of God in our lives—like seasoning on our daily existence—but when it comes to God making the rules (right versus wrong, true versus false, absolutes), we resist. Or many of us prefer to cut and paste God's design for life; it's as if we evaluate the Ten Commandments and decide, "I like commandment numbers 3, 6, 8, and 9, but I think we should throw out the rest."

This is the "god I can control but who does not control me" view, and, in spite of its popularity, it contradicts the biblical presentation of the God who

- authors the Ten Commandments,

- defines Christian character and lifestyle in the Sermon on the Mount (Matthew 5–7),

- claims to be *the* way, *the* truth, and *the* life: the only way of salvation (John 14:6),

■ introduces prophetic words with the statement "Thus says the Lord,"

■ tells us to obey because we have been (through Jesus Christ) "bought at a price" (1 Corinthians 6:20), and

■ promises to answer our prayers if we "remain" in him and obey his commands (John 14:21; 15:7).

In other words, we're not dealing with a "God and me as buddies" equal partnership. We're dealing with a Master-servant, Lord-subject, Creator-created relationship. One of the reasons we squirm in the face of biblical Christianity is because we all want to be gods ourselves; *we* want to make the rules. Such a worldview absolutely contradicts the biblical presentation of Jesus as *Lord of all* to whom we submit.

We submit, but paradoxically, we live in a loving relationship with Jesus Christ. We may not understand all of his purposes in our hardships, but we rest in the fact that he assures us he is with us always. We remember the images of Jesus' suffering on the cross, and we can rest knowing that the almighty God we submit to often works his greater purposes through suffering.

When we don't understand why God is allowing tough things to occur in our lives, is he inviting us to deeper worship? The psalmist exhorts us to worship and bow down, to kneel before the Lord our God, our Maker! The Ten Commandments start off with two commandments that we worship no other than *the one true God*.

The Bible presents God as unique, supreme, worthy of worship, the Creator of everything. To worship "worthless idols" is to make ourselves worthless ourselves (2 Kings 17:15; Psalm 115:4-8; Jeremiah 2:5) because we were created by God to worship him alone!

That's why the writer of Ecclesiastes urges us to come slowly into the presence of God—without a lot of words—because "God is in heaven / and you are on earth; / so let your words be few" (Ecclesiastes 5:2). In other words, prayer is not just barging into God's presence with our shopping list. It's getting quiet and pausing to remember the awesome majesty of the One before whom we enter.

That's why Jesus affirms the sinner who humbly bows and utters "God, be merciful to me, a sinner"—in contrast to the boastful religious leader who in effect says, "God, let me tell you all the reasons that you're fortunate to have me on your team" (Luke 18:9-14).

Worship is getting perspective on who we are in the light of God's awesomeness. Go outside the city and observe the stars. Visit the Grand Canyon. Walk along the ocean (during a storm). Observe the thunderstorm (Psalm 29). Read Psalm 104. God is speaking to remind us of perspective!

What do we do when God acts without explaining? This is obviously the most difficult question as we wrestle with all forms of suffering. *Why God?* echoes in our heads. We know. We've asked it—many times. *Why are people not healed? Why does God allow a perverse, selfish miser to live to ninety-four while a young man full of promise and a generous spirit dies after a painful battle with cancer, or a child dies of leukemia?*

To respond to the specific "Why do the wicked prosper?" we'd refer you to Psalm 73, where the psalmist leaves the questions unresolved as he perceives God's long-term view. The bigger issue pertains to how we understand God. As we grow in our relationship with him, we find ourselves worshiping—not because we understand but because we don't. And we want connection to the Lord who knows our suffering, who wasn't afraid to ask, "Why have you forsaken me?" and who offers us peace *in* the storms (not *from* the storms).

■ Can we ask for the strength to believe even when we don't understand?

■ Can we bring our pain, our tears, and our unanswered prayers before the God who loves us?

■ Can we "sit alone and be silent" (as Jeremiah did) and try to accept the mysterious and unexplained actions of God?

■ Will we ask for grace to worship and bow down before the God whose timing is not ours?

■ Do we accept the fact that—though God is *just*—he simply doesn't administer justice the way we'd like?

These struggles join our sufferings because our Bible tells us that God is Lord over all, but our experience cries out *Why?* Sometimes the best we can do is spend time wrestling with God over those things we don't understand. It may require anger, shouting, crying, pain—but our faith will be stunted until we come before God in honesty about our pain, and then, after wrestling, bow down and echo the words of suffering Job:

Naked I came from my mother's womb
and naked I will depart.
The Lord gave and the Lord has taken away;
may the name of the Lord be praised. (Job 1:21)

Will God use pain to take us outside our comfort zone? When the disciples found themselves in a storm, they first were terrified; then they were angry because Jesus was sleeping through it (Luke 8). "Don't you care that we are perishing?" they asked.

Jesus' response reveals his perspective: "Where is your faith?" In other words, "Don't you believe that I'm going to take care of you?"

This is where our perspective on God most ties into his calling us into the world: Do we really believe that God cares for us? Do we believe he is always with us? Do we believe he wants to fulfill his purposes in our lives—whatever it takes? Are we willing to let him take us outside the comfort zone?

As Hebrews 11 illustrates, faith is only faith when we step into the realm where only God can deliver us. A favorite quotation attributed to Hudson Taylor, pioneer missionary to China in the late nineteenth century, states it this way: "Unless there is an element of risk in our exploits for God, there is no need for faith."

So what do we believe about God—even in the midst of our most difficult situations?

- It affects the way we pray.
- It affects the way we deal with hardships.
- If affects the way we step out into the world as his disciple!

Living with Chronic Pain

In the movie *The Princess Bride*, one of the characters, the Dread Pirate Roberts, drives home a point to the heroine, Princess Buttercup. As she laments the loss of her one true love, he rebukes her self-pity with the statement, "Life is pain, Highness. Anyone who says differently is selling something."

Did you ever feel that way? That life is pain? That the future will be little more than one long emotional, physical, or relational toothache? What possible transformational or positive impact can come when pain seems relentless?

The question usually intensifies as we grow older and our painful experiences move from being acute to being chronic. Acute pain can be severe, but it does go away in a relatively short period of time: we break a bone, a child is caught lying, we cannot manage the household budget, our parents overstay their welcome during the holidays.

But chronic pain—the type that makes us think all of life is pain—drags on without any apparent end in sight. For some, it's physical: the doctor diagnoses rheumatoid arthritis. For others, it's relational:

a daughter announces an out-of-wedlock pregnancy. Some suffer from chronic financial pain: we default on a mountain of debt and lose our home. Others absorb the realities of family pain: our aging parents move in with us.

Acute pain is a night in jail. Chronic pain is a long-term prison sentence without parole. Acute pain cries, "Ouch. I'll never do that again." Chronic pain moans, "Woe is me. I'll never be free again." Although many of us have not suffered actual incarceration, we use the prison analogy because chronic pain is a life situation that is an undesirable condition, circumstance, or relationship that we'd like to escape but have no control over.

In the face of all pain, we start by asking God to heal us. We pray, "Lord, please take away the pain." But what do we do if he doesn't? What do we do with the chronic pain that God leaves untouched?[2]

The Biggest Issue: Choosing to Grow

Viktor Frankl, known for his book *Man's Search for Meaning*, survived Nazi concentration camps in World War II—including Auschwitz. Perhaps his most famous quotation related to his observations in the concentration camps of why some survived—even to the point of generosity in caring for other prisoners—and others shriveled and died. He wrote of those who walked through the concentration camp huts, "comforting others, giving away their last piece of bread. They may have been few in number, but they offer sufficient proof that everything can be taken from a man but one thing: the last of the human freedoms—*to choose one's attitude in any given set of circumstances.*"[3]

Joseph was betrayed by his brothers but he chose to serve Potiphar with excellence, getting him advanced to head house manager. Joseph was betrayed by Potiphar's wife, but he chose to serve in the prison with excellence, getting him advanced to the position of head steward in prison. Joseph was forgotten for two years by the cupbearer, but when he entered into Pharaoh's service, he chose to leave bitterness behind. He served the people of Egypt with excellence, advancing him to the second most powerful position in the Egyptian empire. And when the betraying brothers came to Egypt needing food, Joseph struggled through his own emotions, but he refused to take revenge. He concluded that though the brothers intended evil, God used his suffering to bring about something good—the preservation of the people of Israel (see Genesis 37; 39–50).

Jesus, because of the joy set before him, chose to endure the cross (Hebrews 12:1-3). Stephen chose to look heavenward in the context of being stoned to death after bearing witness to Jesus in front of his assailants, including the vicious persecutor of Christians, Saul of Tarsus.[4] Paul and Silas in prison chose to sing (Acts 16:25). Paul in the Philippian jail chose to rejoice in the Lord.[5]

Father Damien, Belgian missionary to the lepers of Molokai in Hawaii, lives on as a legend of the grace of God to the people of Hawaii. His statue at the capitol building in Honolulu stands as a tribute to his choice to move into a leper colony to serve the people. He served these lepers to the point of his own contraction of and death from leprosy. He chose to enter their suffering, and he went on to suffer and die *with them* so that he might introduce them to the love of the One who suffered and died *for* them.[6]

And consider Joni Eareckson Tada: paralyzed from the neck down from a teenage diving accident, she has begged God for healing. Those prayers were not answered, but her life reflects the choice she made to pray, in effect, "Lord, if you're not going to heal me, then please use my pain for your purposes." She has had a powerful ministry to the world's disabled people and has become one of the foremost Christian advocates for people with physical disabilities. Did God heal her? No. She's struggled through more than fifty years of living as a quadriplegic.[7]

In short, God allows things (experiences, relationships, hardships) in our lives that we would never choose for ourselves, but we can participate in the impact of those actions by the choices we make in response.

E. Stanley Jones served faithfully as a Methodist missionary in India for many years in the twentieth century. He was known for his keen wit, perceptive insights into Indian culture, and effervescent approach to evangelism. In the latter years of his life, he suffered a debilitating stroke that left him unable to speak or walk. Rather than giving up and choosing to wither away into death, Dr. Jones made the decision to claim Jesus as the "Divine Yes" of life and move ahead. He looked to the future through the lens of 2 Corinthians 1:20-22:

> No matter how many promises God has made, they are "Yes" in Christ. And so through him the "Amen" is spoken by us to the glory of God. Now it is God who makes both us and you stand firm in Christ. He anointed us, set his seal of ownership on us, and put his Spirit in our hearts as a deposit, guaranteeing what is to come.

Jones decided to say yes to Jesus and allow him to empower him to confront this stroke. Through a long and challenging recovery, Jones wrote a book (*The Divine Yes*), taught himself to walk and speak again, and returned to his beloved India to preach more than fifty times in the last year of his life. Dr. Jones writes: "It isn't what happens to us that matters, but what we do with what happens to us that counts."[8]

In his book *Creative Suffering*, Christian psychologist Paul Tournier cites a study titled "Orphans Lead the World."[9] The author of the study had reviewed the lives of three hundred historical leaders who were partly or fully orphaned in their childhood. Some we see as great leaders, like biblical Moses or military leaders like Alexander the Great or George Washington. Others we regard as inhuman tyrants like Hitler, Stalin, and Lenin. Tournier observes that "the insecurity consequent upon emotional deprivation must have aroused in these children an exceptional will to power." Tournier uses the study to lay the foundation between deprivation and creativity and to introduce the major premise of his book: When suffering comes, how will we respond? What choices will we make?

The bottom line with hardship and suffering as it pertains to growth and transformation is that we have a choice. To borrow a simplistic phrase, suffering can make us bitter or better. It depends on the long-term choices we make in response to the tough times that come our way.

We do not want to convey the idea that this is an easy process. Words like *struggle*, *ordeal*, *battle*, and *challenge* describe the long-term (sometimes lifetime) process of working through our pains.

A Choice in the Face of Sickness

On a ministry trip to Nigeria, I (Paul) participated in the student missions conference of a university-based group called CASOR, the national student ministry of the Assemblies of God denomination in Nigeria. Toward the end of the conference, the speaker delivered an impassioned challenge to the students to commit themselves to global mission—wherever God would send them.

The response was immediate. Hundreds of students poured toward the stage as an expression of commitment. Some were crying loudly. Others came quietly and pensively. The energy and enthusiasm was palpable.

Reactions to Suffering:
Paul Borthwick's Testimony

The journey of faith can often be more like an emotional roller-coaster ride than a serene walk in the woods—especially when facing chronic hardship and long-term pain. Through the ride, I've observed these emotional reactions in myself and sometimes in others.

- **Anger.** *Why, God, are you letting this happen?* From ages twelve to eighteen, I had been through four surgeries, seven broken bones, and a host of other traumas. When I ruptured the disc in my back at forty-two, I ranted at God: "Enough is enough. I've done my time in physical prison already." He lets us rant—often without responding!

- **Self-pity.** *Poor me. No one knows my sorrows.* After getting diagnosed with diabetes, I saw a pumpkin pie for sale and burst into tears. My wife saw this and said, "But you don't really like pumpkin pie." I replied, "Yeah, but I couldn't eat it even if I wanted to." Self-pity is seldom governed by rationality.

- **Comparison.** *Why do I have to go through this when that other guy gets let off easy?* It's easy to wonder with the psalmist, "Why do the heathen prosper" when God seems to have abandoned us. (Psalms 22, 37, 49, 73, and 88 illustrate that this struggle was real in the lives of the Old Testament writers as well.)

- **Grieving.** *How can I deal with this long-term condition and the corresponding loss of freedom?* A friend's son has had ten surgeries to correct a congenital bone defect in his leg. This surgery seems to have worked, but that young man still faces lots of grieving as he realizes that much of his first eighteen years of life were spent in braces or on crutches.

- **Feeling cheated.** *Is this really the abundant life you promised, Lord?* I remember seeing a T-shirt with the inscription "I prayed the prayer of the prosperity teachers and all I got was this lousy T-shirt." I felt the same way: rather than prosperity, I got a chronic disease.

- **Discouragement.** *I've struggled with this long enough. I quit.* In Psalm 73:2-3 and 13-14, the writer, Asaph, identifies this emotion in himself. He writes words familiar to anyone who has known chronic pain. "My hardships were so great that I almost fell away; I almost quit; I almost abandoned the faith."

Anyone confronting chronic pain, hardship, or suffering will do battle with similar feelings. Family and friends, journaling, reading, prayer, support groups, and counselors all help as we ask God to enable us to deal with our chronic issues and their corresponding impact on our lives.

And over time, we learn to let go of the controls. As I grow and my character is refined, I consciously release my bitterness. I invite God to change my attitude and my perspective on my pain. Some days there is victory; other days it's just a struggle.

Through this emotional roller-coaster ride, sometimes the best I can do is fasten my seat belt of faith, hold on, and trust that God will eventually bring me to the end of the ride where the journey will make sense.[10]

The preacher said a few words to the students, but then he invited a very senior man on the stage, an apostle in the Assemblies of God Church, to come to the microphone and prophesy over the students.

This older saint came forward to address the students. He walked slowly but deliberately. I was in the second row on the stage and noticed that the man had a slight limp, wore glasses, and had a hearing aid in at least one ear. He had obviously logged many miles and years in service to the Lord and the church across Nigeria.

When he came to prophesy, his words were those of great promises. The words sounded a lot like the words of Isaiah 40–43:

- You will rise up on wings like eagles.

- You will walk and not faint.

- Don't be afraid; God is with you wherever you go.

- You will be a light to the nations.

- God will take you through the deep waters.

His prophetic words, full of promises and assurance, continued for several minutes, but my ears perked up when he started the next sentence, *"And sickness . . ."*

Having traveled through Nigeria many times and encountering the impact of the prosperity teaching that exists there, I was fully expecting the man to quote a favorite prosperity phrase from Isaiah. I expected him to say, "And sickness will never touch you because by his stripes we are healed." As we mentioned earlier, prosperity theology often teaches that Jesus not only bore our sins on the cross but in his suffering he took all of our sickness and suffering away as well: "By his wounds we are healed" (Isaiah 53:5). According to the teaching, if we have enough faith, good health will follow and financial success as well. A popular prosperity Nigerian song proclaims it this way: "Me I no go suffer; I no go beg for bread" (*I'm not going to suffer and I'm not going to beg for bread*).

Back to the student mission conference prophecy: this senior apostle surprised me by finishing his prophecy differently. He called out over the students, "and sickness *will not have dominion over you.*"

The phrase leaped out to me. Remember I am a long-term insulin-dependent diabetic—multiple blood tests and injections daily, and the constant need to monitor my food intake. Add to this that in the United States, in Argentina, and again in Nigeria, I have been prayed for and anointed with oil by faith-filled men and women of God who really believe in and were looking for a miraculous healing! We've prayed intently that the diabetes be completely healed. And the miraculous hoped-for answer has never come, at least not yet.

But the Nigerian apostle gave me the prayer that I can always pray: Lord, by the power of the Holy Spirit, I ask that diabetes *not have dominion* over me or my life or my choices.

I went back to the guest house after that service and emailed the apostle's words to many of my friends struggling with chronic issues:

■ To a number of fellow Type 1 diabetics, I e-prayed with them that the daily challenges of diabetes would not have dominion over them.

■ To people doing daily battle with the infirmities of aging (like the apostle—with seeing, hearing and walking challenges), I e-prayed that God would strengthen them to face the challenges of each new day.

■ To a mom and dad living with the pain of their child's mental illness, I e-prayed that their son's infirmity would not have dominion over them.

■ To several suffering through long and painful treatment of various cancers, I e-prayed that their pain would not have dominion over them that day.

The prayer is not a glib panacea. We cannot simply speak to our diseases and hardships and command them to "have no dominion over us" so they disappear like a puff of smoke. I still struggle with high and low blood sugars. My colleagues with cancer can be sick for three days after every chemotherapy treatment. Aging friends can hate their walkers, their hearing aids, and their arthritis. We all struggle with the discouragement that accompanies chronic issues of pain and hardship. Sometimes our hardships do have dominion over us, and we lay on our beds with our faces toward the wall, not knowing how to pray.

The mom and dad I emailed wrote back quickly and thanked me for the exhortation from the apostle. That day their son's mental illness was having dominion over their household, and they were very discouraged. They affirmed that the words about dominion gave them something to pray in the midst of their feelings of helplessness.

They struggled, but they made a choice to see their suffering through eyes of faith. We can make the same choice—to believe that God will take us deeper into dependence on him, will refine our characters, and will transform us more and more into the image of Christ as we grow through our hardships.

Conclusion

When we don't run from suffering, but struggle to persevere faithfully through it, God's kingdom can advance powerfully within us as we become more and more like Jesus. We must never underestimate the impact people who are growing deeply in Christlikeness can make in the world. As Richard Foster has boldly said, "The desperate need today is not for a greater number of intelligent people, or gifted people, but for deep people."[11] Depth, as we have seen, is not easily cultivated apart from suffering. The reason for this can be best understood by distinguishing *training* from *trials* as they pertain to spiritual growth.

Ultimately, spiritual growth can only occur in us by the work of the Holy Spirit. Yet the Scriptures teach us to participate in the Holy Spirit's work of transforming us by training for godliness through the spiritual disciplines (1 Timothy 4:7). Disciplines like prayer, Scripture memorization, silence, solitude, and fasting can enable us to grow in ways that we clearly know we need to grow in. For instance, if I struggle with using my words in a sinful or harmful way, the discipline of silence can strengthen me to have better control of my tongue. When I'm tempted to say something I know I shouldn't, the times I've spent refraining from speaking will enable me to refrain from speaking in the heat of the moment.[12]

While training helps us grow in ways we *know* we need to grow, trials enable us to grow in areas of our lives where we *don't know* we need to grow. Not only is this kind of growth usually unknown but also most often unwanted. Perhaps the reason God allows hardship into our lives as much as he does is because it affords us to become more like Christ in ways we'd never freely choose. The more we become like Jesus through our trials, the more we will be able to be the hands and feet of Jesus to those going through trials of their own. This is the calling of the fellowship of the suffering.

Suffering comes with the territory because God can use our suffering to transform our character into the character of Christ.

Forging Fellowship Reflections

1. Read Psalm 119:67, 71. Looking at your own life, can you describe an experience of suffering (of any form) that shaped you in a positive way? In other words, think of experiences you wish you never had to go through, but when you look back, you can see the positive impact.

2. How can we encourage each other to choose joy in the face of hardship without being trite or superficial?

3. In the list of reactions to suffering, which do you see as most prevalent in yourself?

The Choices We Face—Dynamic Growth or Shriveled Soul

Paul and Christie reflecting at age sixty.

When we were younger, we heard someone say life is the accumulation of one's choices. Now we believe it. We see in ourselves good things and bad that are the result of repeated choices over the days, weeks, months, and years of our lives. We are indeed reaping what we sowed—for good and for ill.

Sometimes this thought scares us, but more recently it has motivated us to start looking at older men and women to examine what choices and patterns have made them what they are.

So far we've noticed two types of prominent patterns in our observations. On the one hand, we notice the vibrant, resilient older folks. These are the people we call "Calebs" because they, like Caleb in the Old Testament (Numbers 13–14; Joshua 14), live to the fullest. They maintain a faith-based optimism, a "give me this mountain" attitude, and a soft heart of gratefulness and servanthood. They have spent a lifetime living out Psalm 119:32—running in the path of God's commandments—so that now they have "enlarged hearts" toward life. We want to be like these people.

But we fear becoming like the other type of person we see. We don't have a personal name for these folks; we just call them shriveled souls (an image we got from a C. S. Lewis novel). Unlike the Calebs, these people never developed the disciplines and attitudes that expand their souls. Rather than demonstrating a spiritual resilience and vitality, they seem withered by life's hardships.

Observing the two types of people, we came up with a list of things we observe about the long-term choices these folks have made concerning character, attitudes, and behavior. We call the list our "Ten Characteristics for Avoiding Shriveled Soul Syndrome." Having observed them, now we're trying to live them out with Caleb-like positive responses, following God wholeheartedly (Joshua 14:8).

1. *Avoid gossip.* Caleb-like people try to find good news about other people. They believe the best rather than assuming the worst. They spread good news about others and avoid judgmental condemnation. Gossip shrinks our souls by diminishing our self-worth because we are living at the expense of others. We build our identity by tearing others down and saying, in effect,

"I may not be much, but at least I'm not as bad as that guy."

2. *Release bitterness.* Bitter people shrivel spiritually as they walk through life under the weight of "apologies owed me." Everyone else is to blame. Caleb took responsibility for his own life (note in the biblical account that there is no record of Caleb or Joshua living the "if only" life). They could have exhausted themselves in bitterness by blaming the ten disbelieving spies ("If only they had believed God, we wouldn't be walking around this stinking wilderness"). They released the people who hurt them and forgave without being asked, and in so doing, they liberated their own souls!

3. *Take risks.* Caleb gave the report, "Let's go for it"; "we can certainly take this land" (Numbers 13:30). The others cowered in fear of exaggerated giants. Expanded souls step out in faith. Shriveled souls run when no one is pursuing. Expanded souls believe God and take risks. Shriveled souls take no risks because they choose to live in fear of what might happen.

4. *Trust.* Living a life of worry guarantees a shrinking soul.

When we try to be God by having everything under control, we shrivel because we cannot bear the weight. Enlarged souls live comfortably with the unknown because they choose to trust God.

5. *Don't live for stuff.* Keep the rampant materialism of our Western world in check. Those who live to accumulate things—either by purchasing these things or by constantly complaining about unfulfilled coveting (which is more likely the case of those of us in ministry)—easily degenerate in shriveled souls.

6. *Master your appetites.* A person controlled by cravings will shrink their spiritual capacity because food, lust, or other unchecked desires will take over. The Caleb person attends to physical as well as spiritual discipline; how else could Caleb have said, "I'm just as strong today as when we left Egypt forty-five years ago" (Joshua 14:11)?

7. *Grow deeply.* Enlarged souls think about the meaning of life. They look for purpose. They struggle to understand and live life based on a philosophical and theological foundation. Shriveled souls get

preoccupied with drivel. They burn up their intellectual energies on monumental facts like sporting scores or the weather, and then find their conversations filled with superficiality.

8. *Be generous.* Stinginess might enlarge our bank accounts, but it shrinks the soul.

9. *Celebrate the past, embrace the present, and anticipate the future.* Enlarged souls learn from the past but don't live there; they recognize that the "good old days" are mostly old. They live today and—like the wife described in Proverbs 31:25 (NASB)—"smile at the future." Shriveled souls dwell in the past, dislike the present, and tremble at the future.

10. *Think globally.* Enlarged souls follow the Lord of the universe. Shriveled souls want a village god who attends to their whims. Enlarged souls celebrate the diversity of God's creation. Shriveled souls want a world just like them. Enlarged souls see their role in serving the world. Shriveled souls make *their* world the whole world.

John Henry Jowett exhorted people to live to God's fullest and to avoid the shriveled soul syndrome. He wrote,

> It is possible to evade a multitude of sorrows through the cultivation of an insignificant life. Indeed, if a person's ambition is to avoid the troubles of life, the recipe is simple: shed your ambitions in every direction, cut the wings of every soaring purpose, and seek a life with the fewest contacts and relations. If you want to get through life with the smallest trouble, you must reduce yourself to the smallest compass. Tiny souls can dodge through life; bigger souls are blocked on every side. As soon as a person begins to enlarge his or her life, resistances are multiplied. Let a person remove petty selfish purposes and enthrone Christ, and sufferings will be increased on every side.[13]

David anticipated an enlarged soul when he stated, "I shall run the way of Your commandments, / For You will enlarge my heart" (Psalm 119:32 NASB). God's people allow him to set their hearts free, and in so doing avoid the shriveled soul syndrome.[14]

Not What I Expected

Joy Through Suffering

*The work of justice, mercy and humility is hard stuff. Yet one of the
fruits of stepping forward into faithful justice is the experience of
joy and deep gladness.*

KENT ANNAN, *SLOW KINGDOM COMING*

WHAT IS THE NATURAL RESPONSE to long-term suffering or
hardship? If we are facing a chronic problem with no apparent solution in sight, how do we react? In our experiences, we've heard
(and even used ourselves) sarcastic or cynical responses like, "The
light at the end of the tunnel is the headlamp of an oncoming train,"
or "They told me, 'Cheer up; things could be worse.' So I cheered
up, and sure enough, things got worse."

Have you ever felt that way? How might you respond?

As followers of Jesus, we sometimes wonder if we would have
embarked on this journey of faith if the earliest words of Jesus we
heard were telling us that as his followers, we would have trials or
tribulations (sufferings) in this world (John 16:33). How would we have
reacted to Paul and Barnabas as they tried to "strengthen" or "encourage me to remain true to the faith" using words like "We must go
through many hardships to enter the kingdom of God" (Acts 14:22)?

When we think of our instinctive human responses to long-term
hardship, we might find ourselves drawn to fatalistic sarcasm or to

escapism (through addictive behaviors we think will numb the pain) or even to the abandonment of our faith.

But then we discover that others have responded differently. Consider again Elisabeth Elliot: after losing one husband as a missionary (killed by the Aucas' spear) and then another to a long-term, painful battle with leukemia, she writes, *"God's ultimate purpose in all suffering is joy."*[1] How could she write that?

How could Nehemiah, writing in the face of insurmountable odds and from the context of exile and oppression, encourage his colleagues: "Do not grieve, for the joy of the LORD is your strength" (Nehemiah 8:10)?

How could Paul and Silas, after being attacked, stripped, beaten, severely flogged, and thrown into the toughest part of a prison, with their feet locked in stocks, start singing hymns (Acts 16:25)? Or how could Paul the apostle again, this time writing from another imprisonment after years of beatings and suffering as an evangelist, encourage his readers, "Rejoice in the Lord always. I will say it again: Rejoice!" (Philippians 4:4)?[2]

Joy: how do we find it in the face of suffering?

Biblical Joy

Ajith Fernando addresses the paradoxical biblical connection of joy and suffering in his book for Christian leaders titled *The Call to Joy and Pain: Embracing Suffering in Your Ministry.* Writing from his own life and ministry context of Sri Lanka, where Christians are a (often persecuted) religious minority (after Buddhists, Hindus, and Muslims), Ajith observes: "Salvation is such an overwhelmingly wonderful blessing that whatever we go through, we always have reason to rejoice." He goes on: "One of the interesting things about the New Testament record is that suffering is hardly ever mentioned without also a mention of the blessings of suffering. And often the blessing mentioned is joy." He notes that joy and suffering are linked in eighteen New Testament texts and then concludes, "Joy and suffering are necessary aspects of Christianity. And they can and must exist together."[3]

How can this be? By understanding what biblical, Christian joy actually is. Dallas Willard defines *joy* as "a pervasive sense of well-being."[4] For we who find our security in Christ, this means that our internal compass can stay steady even when our world quakes around us. Joy, as the Bible illustrates it, does not exclude sorrow or even weeping. Biblical joy is consistent with our confrontation with despair, because with Jesus-based joy, we realize what's really going on and who is really in charge. When we turn to him throughout our biggest disappointments, we find freedom from the god of happiness, because we'll have discovered a joy unshakable. And joy like *this* is what the world is so desperately after.

Circumstance-transcending joy flows from the conviction that God is doing something bigger than we understand. Reflect again on what James writes to his readers, who were suffering first-century persecution:

> Consider it pure joy, my brothers and sisters, whenever you face trials of many kinds, because you know that the testing of your faith produces perseverance. Let perseverance finish its work so that you may be mature and complete, not lacking anything. (James 1:2-4)

Or again, remember how Paul describes the transforming power of hardship when he writes to encourage the believers in Rome:

> Therefore, since we have been justified through faith, we have peace with God through our Lord Jesus Christ, through whom we have gained access by faith into this grace in which we now stand. And we boast in the hope of the glory of God. Not

only so, but we also glory in our sufferings, because we know that suffering produces perseverance; perseverance, character; and character, hope. And hope does not put us to shame, because God's love has been poured out into our hearts through the Holy Spirit, who has been given to us. (Romans 5:1-5)

To these same Roman believers, he reminds them to get past their arguments about dietary issues because "the kingdom of God is not a matter of eating or drinking, but of righteousness, peace and joy in the Holy Spirit" (Romans 14:17). To the Galatians, he listed "joy" as second only to love as a tangible "fruit of the spirit" (Galatians 5:22).

Paul even describes his own emotional state through multiple hardships as "sorrowful, yet always rejoicing; poor, yet making many rich; having nothing, and yet possessing everything" (2 Corinthians 6:10).

Eugene Peterson brilliantly describes this profound dynamic between suffering and joy:

All suffering, all pain, all emptiness, all disappointment, is seed: sow it in God and he will, finally, bring a crop of joy from it. . . . One of the most interesting and remarkable things Christians learn is that laughter does not exclude weeping. Christian joy is not an escape from sorrow. Pain and hardship still come, but they are unable to drive out the happiness of the redeemed.

A common but futile strategy for achieving joy is trying to eliminate things that hurt: get rid of pain by numbing the nerve ends, get rid of insecurity by eliminating risks, get rid of disappointment by depersonalizing your relationships. And then try to lighten the boredom of such a life by buying joy in the form of vacations and entertainment. Christian joy is actualized in the midst of pain, suffering, loneliness and misfortune.[5]

What Peterson is saying boils down to this: although suffering is never to be desired, it can, through fellowship with Christ, open up possibilities for joy that we never thought possible.

Joy in Prison: Lessons from the Apostle Paul

Paul the apostle likely wrote the letter to the Philippians a few weeks or months before he was executed by Nero. He might have been chained in a moldy cell in Rome's Mamertine Prison, from which he also wrote 2 Timothy. If he was writing from this location, these epistles become all the more miraculous. From the dim light of that one oil lamp, Paul was surrounded by dying men, many likely suffering from tuberculosis or pneumonia. Every day, the prison guards would arrive and take inventory. If prisoners had died in the night, the guards would toss their corpses into a hole in the wall that went to a river running under the city. The unnamed prisoners' bodies would wash out to sea.

Imagine writing from that setting and urging the Philippians to "Rejoice in the Lord." Or to his disciple Timothy, writing confidently, "Be strong in the grace that is in Christ Jesus" (2 Timothy 2:1) and "God's word is not chained" (2 Timothy 2:9). Summarizing his own life, Paul wrote with joyful assurance even though he was anticipating his own death: "Now there is in store for me the crown of righteousness, which the Lord, the righteous Judge, will award to me on that day" (2 Timothy 4:8).

The Philippian letter may have been written from another, less-severe form of imprisonment. It might be that Paul was under house arrest in Rome, chained to a Roman guard 24/7, without freedom of movement or privacy.

Whatever the context, the question remains: How did Paul maintain his faith, his attitude, his joy, and his perseverance in the face of such hardship and suffering? And more related to ourselves, how can we rediscover joy, especially joy in the face of hardship? The easiest thing for most of us is to live with a spirit of joyless toleration. Or our lives are characterized by the up-and-down roller-coaster ride of emotion, ranging from great joy to extreme discouragement, disillusionment, or sorrow.

But how can we discover steady, unwavering joy?

To lead us in our investigation of joy, let's turn our attention to Paul's letter to the Philippians, Paul's most joy-filled letter. "Joy is the music of Philippians" with at least fourteen references to *joy* or *rejoice* in four short chapters.

As noted already, we remember that Paul is writing from prison:

- "I am in chains." (Philippians 1:7)

- "Because of my chains." (Philippians 1:14)

- Perhaps he was on the Roman equivalent of death row and awoke every day without knowing if it would be his last—"so that . . . Christ will be exalted in my body, whether by life or by death." (Philippians 1:20)

- The phrase "For to me, to live is Christ and to die is gain" echoes the view of someone whose death is soon to come. (Philippians 1:21)

What's Your Prison?

Before examining Philippians, let's define *prison*. Though few of us might ever suffer the horrors of actual imprisonment for our faith, as our Christian family does in some locales, let's use *prison* as a metaphor. Consider prison as any undesirable circumstance or reality in our lives that we would change if we could, but we are powerless to overcome. So by way of review of the variety of prisons we could face, let's ask, what is *your* prison?

■ *Physical* limitations? Suffering? Sickness? Chronic illness? Burnout? Exhaustion? Physical handicap?

■ *Relational* prison? Interpersonal conflict? An intolerable boss? A rebellious child? An unreasonably demanding parent? Care for aging parents? An unsaved relative? An abusive spouse?

■ *Emotional pain?* Disappointment that life is not turning out as expected? Loneliness? Fear of the future? Past or present hurts that simply will not go away?

■ *Spiritual* prison? An unsaved spouse who mocks you when you read the Bible? Spiritual opposition from family or friends who think that you are following Christ in some sort of cult?

■ *Economic* prison? Debt from college? Long-term unemployment or underemployment? Credit card debt?

Do you face a prison-like challenge in your life? Are these things crushing your ability to experience joy? Do you believe you could actually experience joy in your prison?

While Paul the apostle might not have experienced the exact kinds of hardship you might be going through, he was acquainted with suffering on many levels. Consider his résumé. Contrasting himself to his detractors, he summarizes his credentials in 2 Corinthians 11:23-28:

> Are they servants of Christ? (I am out of my mind to talk like this.) I am more. I have worked much harder, been in prison more frequently, been flogged more severely, and been exposed to death again and again. Five times I received from the Jews the forty lashes minus one. Three times I was beaten with rods, once I was pelted with stones, three times I was shipwrecked, I spent a night and a day in the open sea, I have been constantly on the move. I have been in danger from

rivers, in danger from bandits, in danger from my fellow Jews, in danger from Gentiles; in danger in the city, in danger in the country, in danger at sea; and in danger from false believers. I have labored and toiled and have often gone without sleep; I have known hunger and thirst and have often gone without food; I have been cold and naked. Besides everything else, I face daily the pressure of my concern for all the churches.

In 2 Corinthians 6:4-10, Paul says,

Rather, as servants of God we commend ourselves in every way: in great endurance; in troubles, hardships and distresses; in beatings, imprisonments and riots; in hard work, sleepless nights and hunger; in purity, understanding, patience and kindness; in the Holy Spirit and in sincere love; in truthful speech and in the power of God; with weapons of right-eousness in the right hand and in the left; through glory and dishonor, bad report and good report; genuine, yet regarded as impostors; known, yet regarded as unknown; dying, and yet we live on; beaten, and yet not killed; sorrowful, yet always rejoicing; poor, yet making many rich; having nothing, and yet possessing everything.

Paul the apostle knew all sorts of prisons:

- *physical* suffering unlike anything most of us will ever endure
- *emotional drain* from caring for people and from facing constant opposition from enemies
- *relational pain* from people who deserted him, people who opposed him (Philippians 1), and people who disappointed him
- *spiritual opposition*—both human and demonic
- *economic hardship*, living often on the edge of poverty

So how did Paul do it? How did he find joy—even in the midst of prison?

Paul Believed God Was in Control

Paul believed in the sovereignty of God—that God is ultimately in control even when we don't understand the how or why of our circumstances. Paul found joy because he saw God's hand in every circumstance. He writes by way of introducing his imprisoned reality:

> I want you to know, brothers and sisters, that what has happened to me has actually served to advance the gospel. As a result, it has become clear throughout the whole palace guard and to everyone else that I am in chains for Christ. And because of my chains, most of the brothers and sisters have become confident in the Lord and dare all the more to proclaim the gospel without fear. (Philippians 1:12-14)

Paul knew God was using his chains to advance the gospel by both enabling the Roman prison guards to hear the gospel and by encouraging the other Christians to remain faithful and be bold.

Paul's spirit is reminiscent of Joseph's response to his brothers: "You meant evil against me, but God meant it for good" (Genesis 50:20 ESV). Joseph had been abandoned, betrayed, imprisoned, and forgotten—but now he acknowledged that all of this transpired under the sovereign hand of God to save the people of Israel.

Prison in whatever form is ultimately loss of control. Something or someone has taken over the reins of our lives. Our natural and normal human tendency is to fight, resist, and try to escape. But when escape becomes impossible, then what?

One of the first mentors and spiritual fathers in my (Paul) life was Ernie Tavilla. Ernie had a simple, beautiful faith. Charismatic and Pentecostal in every sense of these words, Ernie loved to pray for the miraculous—including healing. He hosted and sponsored faith healers to minister in Boston. He took me to Jesus Rallies (this was the early 1970s when the Jesus Movement was moving across America) where former heroin addicts and demon-possessed people testified of Holy Spirit deliverance. Ernie opened my eyes to believing in faith like that of the early church in the book of Acts.

Later in his life and mine, however, I learned an even deeper lesson from Ernie. In his sixties, Ernie contracted cancer. Faith-filled prayers for healing went out globally through Ernie's amazing network of contacts. If faith alone could heal, Ernie should have been raised up. But he wasn't. The cancer finally took his life.

Before he died, Ernie taught me about total abandonment to the sovereign will of God. From his hospital bed he said, "Paul, I don't think God is going to heal me this time. I think God has me here on this cancer floor to bear witness to the saving power of Jesus Christ. There are people here who have no hope of eternal life, and I'm here to share it." At his funeral, the preaching pastor reported on the people from that cancer floor who had put their trust in Jesus before they died—because Ernie allowed God to use his prison to proclaim hope.

In his commentary about the book of Philippians, Stuart Briscoe writes,

> To rejoice in the Lord does not mean to ignore your responsibilities; neither does it mean to evade obvious issues. Rather, it means to be fully cognizant of the situation, fully prepared to deal with it responsibly, and fully convinced of the power of the Lord to give you wisdom, grace and courage to deal with whatever comes along.
>
> When this attitude is adopted it will not produce a giddy irresponsibility or a naive ecstasy, but a deep, mature, responsible faith that has as its core a majestic Lord. When He

is the One at the core, joy can result because of the certainty of his ultimate triumph, the assurance of his benevolent purpose and the opportunities for spiritual growth that the situation affords.[6]

Acknowledging that God is in control is one of the primary functions of prayer. That's why Paul exhorted the Philippians to turn their anxieties into opportunity to pray. He wrote, "Do not be anxious about anything, but in every situation, by prayer and petition, with thanksgiving, present your requests to God. And the peace of God, which transcends all understanding, will guard your hearts and your minds in Christ Jesus" (Philippians 4:6-7). Prayer acknowledges that God is in control. Anxiety forgets that God is there, and we try to take control ourselves.

Among our most amazing experiences of seeing this type of joy has come when visiting fellow believers in places like Haiti and Bangladesh, where many suffer under the weight of long-term economic hardship. Or Lebanon and Angola, where we visited churches in the midst of their civil wars. Or Sri Lanka and Nepal, as they and their nations worked to recover from a tsunami and an earthquake. We have been awed and inspired while worshiping with believers lifting their voices in praise, even through the tears of their ongoing pain.

Paul's Joy Flowed Out of His Convictions

We referred to choosing our attitudes earlier (chap. 5). Paul found joy in prison because he lived by conviction rather than by his outward circumstances. His joy was based on internal belief rather than external conditions, and as a result he had a joy that transcended his suffering, his prison, and any feelings of helplessness he might have drifted toward. This explains his words to the Corinthian believers: "We know sorrow, yet our joy is inextinguishable" (2 Corinthians 6:10 Phillips).

When telling the Philippian believers that his opponents were using his imprisonment as a reason to criticize him, Paul wrote,

> It is true that some preach Christ out of envy and rivalry, but others out of goodwill. The latter do so out of love, knowing that I am put here for the defense of the gospel. The former preach Christ out of selfish ambition, not sincerely, supposing that they can stir up trouble for me while I am in chains. But what does it matter? The important thing is that in every way, whether from false motives or true, Christ is preached. And because of this I rejoice. (Philippians 1:15-18)

This is the difference between joy and happiness. *Happiness* derives from the same word as "happen," "happening," or "happenstance." Happiness fluctuates with what happens. Conviction is a choice—to rejoice beyond our feelings or emotions, or better, through them. I (Paul) like to tell myself that by the power of the Holy Spirit, I can choose an attitude of gratitude.

When Paul tells the Philippians to set their minds on things that are true, noble, right, pure, lovely, admirable, excellent, or praiseworthy (Philippians 4:8), he is telling them to make a choice. He goes on to illustrate by describing his responses to the variations in his own life:

> I am not saying this because I am in need, for I have learned to be content whatever the circumstances. I know what it is to be in need, and I know what it is to have plenty. I have learned the secret of being content in any and every situation, whether well fed or hungry, whether living in plenty or in want. I can do all this through him who gives me strength. (Philippians 4:11-13)

Observing Paul's joy in the face of hardship, Ajith Fernando writes, "The happiest people in the world are not those who have no suffering—they are those who are not afraid of suffering."[7]

When confronting a large or small prison-like challenge in our own lives, we like to ask ourselves, *Do I want to be a thermostat or a thermometer?* A thermometer person (in our self-dialogue) reports the temperature; a thermostat person determines the temperature. A thermometer person reports that the local Christian fellowship is unfriendly, whereas a thermostat person starts the welcoming committee. A thermometer person complains about the boss; a thermostat person dedicates time each day to pray for the boss.

When Paul writes that he has "learned to be content in any and all circumstances" (paraphrase), he is referring to the God-given strength to be that kind of thermostat person: to sing in prison, to share his faith in prison, and to celebrate the hand of God in his life, even while in prison. This is what Paul means when he writes, "I can do all things through Christ who strengthens me."

He is saying, in effect, "By the power of Jesus at work in me, I can choose joy."

May the Lord give us strength to live this way!

Paul's Joy Pointed Toward Heaven

In our age of desired comfort and long-term happiness, we often forget to view our hardships through an eternal perspective. In contrast, Paul sets the example of sustained joy—even in his various prisons—because he lived with eternity in mind. He lived in a way that illustrated the psalmist's words that "weeping may stay for the night, but rejoicing comes in the morning" (Psalm 30:5).

For Paul, that morning was his ultimate eternal reward. He believed in heaven, in heavenly reward, and in the final goal of his salvation. He really believed that "our light and momentary troubles are achieving for us an eternal glory that far outweighs them all" (2 Corinthians 4:17).

He believed that "to live is Christ and to die is gain" (Philippians 1:21) and that he was pressing on "toward the goal to win the prize for which God has called me heavenward in Christ Jesus (Philippians 3:14).

No one in the New Testament wrote about heaven more than Paul, and he lived with his ultimate, heavenly destination in mind. He consistently took risks with his security in preaching the gospel, because he saw his citizenship in heaven (Philippians 3:20). He taught that the sufferings of this life were nothing compared to the glory of heaven (2 Corinthians 4:17). His mission endeavors were motivated by heaven, and he went anywhere in obedience to the Lord of heaven, Jesus Christ.

Facing persecutions in Jerusalem, he told the Ephesian elders, "I only know that in every city the Holy Spirit warns me that prison and hardships are facing me. However, I consider my life nothing to me, my only aim is to finish the race and complete the task the Lord Jesus has given me—the task of testifying to the good news of God's grace" (Acts 20:23-24). To the Romans, he established his sense of priorities based on his heavenly destination: "None of us lives for ourselves alone and no one dies for ourselves alone. If we live, we live for the Lord; and if we die, we die for the Lord. So, whether we live or die, we belong to the Lord" (Romans 14:7-8). And his life exhorts us to follow his example: "Set your minds on things above, not on earthly things. For you died, and your life is now hidden with Christ in God" (Colossians 3:2-3).

Paul is saying, "In light of the awesome future promised by God to those who follow Jesus Christ, we can live effectively and courageously in the present!" In contrast to the modern world where we run from death and try to deny its reality, Paul lived with eternity in mind, and he made his decisions accordingly. And, in contrast to our world where we often think about heaven only for comfort after we've lost loved ones, Paul wrote about heaven primarily to challenge the lives of those of us who are alive!

Paul reminds the Philippians that he sees his entire life as a mission toward eternity:

> Not that I have already obtained all this, or have already arrived at my goal, but I press on to take hold of that for which Christ Jesus took hold of me. Brothers and sisters, I do not consider myself yet to have taken hold of it. But one thing I do: Forgetting what is behind and straining toward what is ahead, I press on toward the goal to win the prize for which God has called me heavenward in Christ Jesus. (Philippians 3:12-14)

We have to ask, did Paul have an escapist attitude? Some sort of warped spiritualized death wish? In no way. Paul was simply living the way God wants all of us to live: remembering that this life is a precious gift, but this life is not all there is. His joy was sustained because he knew that the hardships of today were minimal compared to the ultimate destination, the glory of God in heaven. Thus Paul writes to the Corinthians,

> Therefore we do not lose heart. Though outwardly we are wasting away, yet inwardly we are being renewed day by day. For our light and momentary troubles are achieving for us an eternal glory that far outweighs them all. So we fix our eyes not on what is seen, but on what is unseen, since what is seen is temporary, but what is unseen is eternal. (2 Corinthians 4:16-18)

Paul lived in direct contrast to many of us who want to find total fulfillment in this life, who resist hardship because we want comfort first (not Jesus first). If we think that

- this life is all there is,

- that long life and comfort are our "rights,"

- that Jesus' return might interrupt our long-term plans,

- *then* we become self-centered and preoccupied with protecting our lives.

But when we live with a firm conviction about heaven,

- we find strength to endure hardship,

- we find courage to sacrifice temporal pleasures in exchange for heavenly rewards, and

- we find strength to live by eternal values.

From Paul's Life to Ours

Thankfully, most of us reading Paul's words do not find ourselves facing the hardships he faced, but that doesn't minimize the large or small prisons we might be facing. How does Paul's example translate into our lives? What does it mean for us to release ourselves to the sovereignty of God? How do we choose joy in spite of our circumstances? Where does heavenly reward fit into the way we live every day?

Obviously, there are no easy answers or trite solutions, but Paul's example challenges us again to remember that suffering does indeed come with the territory of following Jesus. His example reminds us to pray through our hardships—both that God will use them and that we will be strengthened to be content in all circumstances. His eternal outlook reminds us that this life is not all there is; in the words of the spiritual, "soon we be over with da troubles of the world, we're going home to live with God."

Joni Eareckson Tada provides powerful words of encouragement from her wheelchair:

Many people in the throes of suffering, disappointment, and despair, feel utterly stuck in their circumstances. They see no hope beyond their day-to-day drudgery of disability routines; but when hurting families place themselves under the shower of God's mercy, suddenly the clouds part. They realize there's hope, life, and even joy beyond their suffering.[8]

Conclusion

Only a small minority ever really expect to suffer as a result of following Christ. But even fewer of us could imagine experiencing the inexpressible joy that accompanies suffering with and for Jesus. While this kind of joy is nearly impossible to put into words, it can be visibly seen and tangibly felt in the midst of believers of who are "rejoicing because they had been counted worthy of suffering" for Christ (Acts 5:41). This kind of rejoicing forges fellowship that cannot be broken, and faith that cannot be deterred. For in sharing Christ's sufferings alongside his church, we experience the blessings that come in knowing that while our bodies may be beaten or our souls may be crushed or our lives even taken, great is our reward in heaven (Matthew 5:11-12). "Rejoice and be glad!"

So no matter what prison you might find yourself in, no bars are thick enough, no chains are strong enough, no cells are dark enough to lock the joy of Jesus out. In fellowship with our unstoppable God is the "fullness of joy" that can never be shaken, no matter what or who is taken from us (Psalm 16:11 ESV).

Though suffering comes with the territory, suffering can also give birth to unbreakable joy.

Forging Fellowship Reflections

1. If the metaphor of "prison" is used to describe any situation or circumstance that we can't change but would if we could, what are your perceived prisons?

2. In the face of these prisons, how can we encourage each other to be thermostats rather than thermometers?

3. Why do you think we hear so little in our churches or from popular Christian leaders about knowing Jesus through the fellowship of the suffering?

PART THREE

fellowship
with others

It's Our Family

Solidarity Through Suffering

Join with me in suffering, like a good soldier of Christ Jesus.

APOSTLE PAUL (2 TIMOTHY 2:3)

ONE OF OUR (Paul and Christie) most unforgettable journeys took us to northern Mozambique shortly after their twenty-year civil war had ended. We went to visit (and hopefully encourage) a couple supported by our church who were serving there. Our brief visit gave us only a glimpse into the hardships of the life they willingly endured so the Bible translation could be completed in one of the local languages: power outages, food shortages, minimal medical care, limited mobility, dangers from robbers, and remnant rebels who roamed the countryside as armed fugitives.

When we were departing, we asked the couple what message they wanted us to report back home to our church. They responded immediately with a Scripture reference: "2 Corinthians 1:10-11. Tell the church 2 Corinthians 1:10-11."

We had to look up the passage. It's Paul's words to the Corinthians concerning the hardships he was facing:

[God] has delivered us from such a deadly peril, and he will deliver us again. On him we have set our hope that he will continue to deliver us, as you help us by your prayers. Then many will give thanks on our behalf for the gracious favor granted us in answer to the prayers of many.

Our friends were asking us and our church for solidarity. "Don't forget us. Remember our challenges. Pray for us in the face of our hardships. We trust God to work even in the face of these difficulties—as you our fellow believers help us by your prayers."

They were, in effect, asking us to enter their suffering with them.

Heart Connection Through Suffering

We find encouragement when someone else hears our story of suffering or hardship and comes alongside. Even the words *empathy* (to feel with) or *compassion* (to suffer with) remind us of the longing we all have that someone else would understand what we are going through.

The solidarity in suffering explains the success of the Alcoholics Anonymous movement (or other addictive-behavior movements). People addicted to alcohol (or something else) find themselves strengthened to resist their addictions because they have found a loving fellowship with people who understand what they are going through. Elisabeth Elliot states it succinctly: "Those who speak most deeply to our hearts in times of trouble are invariably those who have suffered."[1]

Applied to us in the wider Christian community, our suffering gives us the potential not only to form deeper fellowship within the church but also an immovable solidarity with Christ. Shared opposition and suffering often help us get past some of our lesser differences. Persecution often unites the church and extends the potential growth of the church.

Several years ago, when twenty-five Coptic Orthodox Egyptian Christians were brutally martyred by beheading in Libya, it brought the entire Christian community together—Catholic, Orthodox, and Protestant. The jihadist killers videotaped the brutal death of these workers to instill fear in the Christian community. Instead, the testimony of those who died was recorded too, and their proclamation of loyalty to Jesus Christ fueled greater courage in the Egyptian church.

Elam Ministries, dedicated to equipping the church in Iran, published a similar story titled "Backfired" in which they described the growth of the Christian church in Iran from five hundred two decades ago to hundreds of thousands today. Why? The church's response to persecution. A Chinese pastor reports at a conference, "In China the government has stopped imprisoning us because every time they send us to prison, they create a hero." *Christianity Today* reports that the church in India is "outpacing persecution" because the church has been emboldened by the opposition. Karen Ellis, observing the strength of Christians facing anti-Christian hostility in the Middle East, summarizes this fellowship of the suffering: "They answer to this hostility with what I describe as 'productive perseverance working through community.' They are filled with deep hope in Christ that drives out fear of man, and their lives are often marked by radical personal transformation and a communal discipleship that is so attractive that others risk stigmatization to know it."[2]

Solidarity with Others Who Suffer

Suffering together strengthened the church in its earliest days. When the apostles received threats from the religious leaders of the day, they returned to the Christian community to pray. Luke records the result: "After they prayed, the place where they were meeting was shaken. And they were all filled with the Holy Spirit and spoke the word of God boldly" (Acts 4:31).

They were threatened together, which led to prayer together. God answered, and they were touched and empowered together by the power of the Holy Spirit.

Suffering in all of its various forms is part of the discipleship process. It can deepen our joy, transform our growth, extend our mission, intensify our prayers, and fuel our passion. Altogether, suffering can bind us in deep community so that we understand that "if one part hurts, every other part is involved in the hurt, and in the healing" (1 Corinthians 12:26 *The Message*).

Paul writes to the Corinthians that suffering can be a tool to equip us to care for others—both within and outside the Christian community:[3]

> Praise be to the God and Father of our Lord Jesus Christ, the Father of compassion and the God of all comfort, who comforts us in all our troubles, so that we can comfort those in any trouble with the comfort we ourselves receive from God. For just as we share abundantly in the sufferings of Christ, so also our comfort abounds through Christ. (2 Corinthians 1:3-5)

Because we share in carrying each other's burdens (Galatians 6:2), we can turn our personal pain into opportunities to care for others. Moreover, God often allows us to go through severe trials so we can come alongside others when they are grieving and hurting.

But once again we remind ourselves that growth through suffering isn't easy, and we will be faced constantly with how to respond. Christie's mom went through a barrage of physical suffering that involved a fall, surgery, complications, an amputation, and over seven months in the hospital. The entire ordeal left her wheelchair bound, never to walk again. Nevertheless, she demonstrated remarkable resilience. One particularly difficult day, however, she made this humorous but sobering statement: "I know that other people have it tougher than me, but the fact that other people are suffering worse isn't helping me today."

Christie's mom illustrates that suffering by itself doesn't make us better at caring for others. In fact, suffering can result in a despairing loneliness. But if we continue to engage in the challenge of embracing suffering for growth, it can enable us to care for others "with the same comfort we've received from God."

When I (Paul) was told by my doctors that I had Type 1 diabetes, I knew it meant that (barring miraculous healing), I was looking at a lifetime regimen of daily blood tests, insulin shots and food control. We called our long-time friend Carolyn. She and her husband, Donald, had gone to university with me, and we had served our church's youth ministry together. I had performed their wedding. But above all, I called Carolyn because I knew that she had lived with Type 1 diabetes since she was eight years old. She'd know what we were going through. She made time to see us, explained everything from blood tests to low blood sugars to some what-to-expect predictions concerning why diabetics should probably not eat pizza! We were together with Carolyn and Donald in a fellowship of the suffering, and she was comforting us with the comfort she had received from God.

Several months after starting on the regimen of shots, tests, and a carbohydrate-managed diet, I saw Christie telling people about the challenges of managing the diabetes lifestyle. Referring to our "old life" versus our "new life," I overheard her say, "All that changed when *we* got diabetes." I almost broke into tears. She had willingly entered into solidarity with me—even though she didn't have the disease.

Speaking of Christie, I've watched her minister with compassion to people who have pain in their family relationships, because Christie is allowing God to use her pain to care for others. She's listened with compassionate understanding to one Christian brother as he described the pain of not being able to help his mentally ill child; Christie understands because she grew up with a mentally ill brother. She's empathized with a high school student who has just learned that her mother is an alcoholic; Christie was a teenager when she learned her mother was an alcoholic. And she's come alongside a friend who fears for the future of her mentally handicapped daughter, because Christie is the guardian for her younger mentally handicapped sister.

The basis of this book stems from this idea of fellowship in suffering. When I (Paul) first heard Dave preach, I could tell there was a depth in him that only suffering could have forged. Even though he was chronologically relatively young, he had the testimony of someone who knew the potential of an inescapable prison.

The couple we visited in Mozambique later experienced a devastating loss when their six-year-old daughter died from cerebral malaria. We thought they would return home overwhelmed by the loss. They persevered and stayed on to serve. When I inquired as to where they found the strength, they shared that when they buried their daughter, they were surrounded by four Mozambican pastors— all had also buried at least one of their own children.

Suffering forges solidarity with others like nothing else can. There is no community on earth like the fellowship of the suffering.

Solidarity with the Suffering Church

From a biblical perspective, our brothers and sisters who suffer because of Christ constitute a critical calling for all members of the church to stand alongside them. The writer of Hebrews urges us to "continue to remember those in prison as if you were together with them in prison, and those who are mistreated as if you yourselves were suffering" (Hebrews 13:3). Peter wrote to Christians facing persecution by reminding them to "be alert and of sober mind. Your enemy the devil prowls around like a roaring lion looking for someone to devour. Resist him, standing firm in the faith, *because you know that the family of believers throughout the world is under-going the same kind of sufferings"* (1 Peter 5:8-9, emphasis added).

Over years of involvement in global mission, I (Paul) have changed my perspective on the sufferings of the church around the world. I formerly talked about the persecuted church or the economically impoverished church or the church in the face of disasters (like floods, earthquakes, and hurricanes). My references were usually in us-and-them language: "They are going through this or that, and we need to respond."

After many travels, visits to refugee camps, witnessing poverty and suffering unlike anything I've actually faced in my comfortable Western lifestyle, and then reflecting on the phrase "If one member suffers, all suffer together with it," I've change the way I describe things. For me, it's no longer "the church" that is suffering. Instead, it's *my family,* or *our family* that is suffering.

- It's our family who lives in the dangerous Kibera slums of Nairobi.

- It's our family wandering as exiles from the wars in Iraq or Syria.

- It's our family—often on both sides of the violence—in Israel and Palestine.

- It's our family suffering under the brutal regime in North Korea.

- It's our family in Iran or India or Pakistan or in a variety of other locales.

- It's our family in the anti-Christian hostility of some secular universities in America or Europe.

But let's be honest: ultimately the first and worst suffering that any of us face is our own. If we have a headache or financial woes or a difficult boss, our God-designed instinct for self-preservation turns our concern inward—toward our own pain. Take heart, even Jesus, in his greatest moments of suffering on the cross, was conscious of his own physical pain ("I thirst") and his spiritual/emotional feelings of desertion by his heavenly Father ("Why have you forsaken me?"). But Jesus went beyond his own pain to care for the thief who asked for mercy, for his now abandoned mother, and for his killers, who needed forgiveness.

This is the challenge we face in the midst of our own various sufferings: Can we ask God for the grace to get past ourselves to care for others in pain?

Solidarity with Christ

Suffering does not guarantee deeper fellowship with fellow Christians. Too many times in our comfort-oriented Western culture, the person in pain feels isolated and alone. Our "fellowship" groups prefer not to focus on the unanswered prayers of the chronically ill or the suffering laments of the person in pain. We all would love to be in fellowship groups where the prisons of life bonded us closer together, but it isn't always so. Even in some of the countries cited earlier (like Egypt or Iran), suffering Christians mourn the fact that their wealthier friends fled their countries to move to Europe or North America.

So what do we do when we find ourselves sighing with the words of the spiritual—"Nobody knows the trouble I've seen. Nobody knows my sorrow"?

We need to go back to Philippians 3:10 and remember that the fellowship of the suffering Paul was referring to was first and foremost fellowship with Jesus himself. Paul writes from his own captive isolation, "I want to know Jesus." Biblical scholar William Barclay observes that the verb *know* "indicates the most intimate knowledge of another person. It is not Paul's aim to know about Christ, but personally to know him."[4] Barclay explains that to know

Christ involves both the power of the resurrection and, mysteriously, the fellowship of sharing in his sufferings: "To suffer for the faith is not a penalty, it is a privilege, for thereby we share in the very work of Christ. . . . To know Christ means that we share the way He walked; we share the Cross He bore; we share the death He died; and finally we share the life He lives forevermore."[5]

The believers and writers in the New Testament knew this reality because they understood suffering as a cherished way to be identified with their crucified Savior.

■ After rebukes and floggings, "the apostles left the Sanhedrin, rejoicing because they had been counted worthy of suffering disgrace for the Name" (Acts 5:41).

■ To comfort the Roman believers, Paul writes to assure them of Christ's presence in their own sufferings:

What, then, shall we say in response to these things? If God is for us, who can be against us? He who did not spare his own Son, but gave him up for us all—how will he not also, along with him, graciously give us all things? Who will bring any charge against those whom God has chosen? It is God who justifies. Who then is the one who condemns? No one. Christ Jesus who died—more than that, who was raised to life—is at the right hand of God and is also interceding for us. Who shall separate us from the love of Christ? Shall trouble or hardship or persecution or famine or nakedness or danger or sword? As it is written:

"For your sake we face death all day long;
    we are considered as sheep to be slaughtered."

No, in all these things we are more than conquerors through him who loved us. For I am convinced that neither death nor life, neither angels nor demons, neither the present nor the future, nor any powers, neither height nor depth, nor anything else in all creation, will be able to separate us from the love of God that is in Christ Jesus our Lord. (Romans 8:31-39)

▨ To authenticate his own ministry, Paul appealed to his physical identification with Jesus' sufferings: "I carry on my scarred body the marks [*stigmata*] of my owner, the Lord Jesus" (Galatians 6:17, Phillips).

▨ Paul writes that his sufferings are a continuation of the sufferings of Christ (Colossians 1:24).

▨ Paul writes from prison to encourage Timothy to accept suffering as part of the Christ-following life. "Do not be ashamed of the testimony about our Lord or of me his prisoner. Rather, join with me in suffering for the gospel, by the power of God" (2 Timothy 1:8).

▨ Peter urges Christians to persevere in the face of suffering because "to this you were called, because Christ suffered for you, leaving you an example, that you should follow in his steps" (1 Peter 2:21).

In a discussion with an Egyptian pastor, I (Paul) asked him about the role of dreams and visions in helping Muslims turn to Jesus. He told many stories, but then his wife added, "Sometimes Jesus appears to them after they become Christians too—to encourage them in the face of suffering." She went on, "A young, formerly Muslim man had committed his life to Christ. When his older brother found out, he started beating him down with a rod. The young man looked up and saw Jesus, and Jesus showed him the scars in his hands. The young man knew that Jesus was saying, 'I endured this for you; please endure this for Me.'"

Amy Carmichael, Irish missionary to India for fifty-five years, experienced a life-altering fall that left her a bedridden invalid for almost half of those years in India. Yet from that bed she led the Dohnavur Fellowship and the ministry of rescuing girls from being sold into prostitution in the Hindu temples. It is said that Amy Carmichael had two framed prints in her bedroom. The first simply said "Be Still," an obvious reference to Psalm 46:10, "Be still, and know that I am God." The second had the words, "I know," an allusion to the comfort Amy drew from the reality that Jesus had suffered himself.

Amy Carmichael exemplified through her life and writings encouragement for perseverance in suffering. Her poem "No Scar?" challenges us to consider our own willingness to find our solidarity with Christ, asking, "Can he have followed far/Who hast no wound or scar?[6]"

Listen to the Voice of the Persecuted

According to the Center for the Study of Global Christianity, an estimated 900,000 Christians were martyred between 2005 and 2015—an estimated 90,000 per year.[7] With that in mind, we need to know how to engage in solidarity prayer for our global family. What follows is designed to help us to know how to think and pray by listening to the voice of someone who knows persecution.

In the early years of the twenty-first century, the church in Sri Lanka endured tremendous persecution at the hands of radical Buddhist extremists who were bent on driving the Christian church out. They wanted the Western influence of Christianity gone so the country could be completely Buddhist. (They also persecuted Hindus and Muslims during this time.)

A long-term colleague, Pastor Adrian De Visser, leads a ministry in Sri Lanka called Kithu Sevana, which in the Sinhalese (majority) language of Sri Lanka means "In the Shadow of the Cross." When we think of solidarity with our persecuted family around the world, Adrian's teaching (written in 2004 at the height of extreme religious persecution in Sri Lanka) helps us know how to pray. The ideas that follow are excerpted from a talk he gave to his Kithu Sevana team, which later appeared in a newsletter he sent to his global network. As he challenged his colleagues, he offers us fuel for prayer for our faith family that suffers throughout the world:

- He challenges them not to be surprised or shrink away in fear, intimidated by the realities of persecution. When we pray for our persecuted family, let's always ask God to grant them strength, courage, and an assurance of his presence with them.

- He reminds them not be surprised by suffering but to remember Jesus' victory. He writes, "After all, Jesus warned us about the very real possibility of persecution (in John 15:20-21; Matt. 10:24-25). . . . But Jesus did not simply leave us with a warning, he also assured us that the Gates of Hell shall not prevail against us (Matt. 16:18)." Let's pray that our persecuted family remembers Jesus' ultimate victory.

- He urges them to draw strength from Christian history with stories like these: "During China's Boxer Rebellion of 1900, insurgents captured a mission station, blocked all the gates but one, and in front of that one gate placed a cross flat on the ground. Then the word was passed to those inside that any who trampled the cross underfoot would be permitted their freedom and life, but that any refusing would be shot. Terribly frightened, the first seven students trampled the cross under their feet and were allowed to go free. But the eighth student, a young girl, refused to commit the sacrilegious act.

Kneeling beside the cross in prayer for strength, she arose and moved carefully around the cross, and went out to face the firing squad. Strengthened by her example, every one of the remaining ninety-two students followed her to the firing squad." Pray that the persecuted remember and draw strength from the great crowd of witnesses and martyrs who have preceded them (Hebrews 12:1-3).

■ He gives them an overview of all of the benefits that result from suffering: purification of the church, increased prayer, greater unity in the church, powerful testimony to the persecutors, heightened awareness of Christ's accompanying presence, and even revival. Let's ask God to help those facing persecution or hardship for their faith to remember the long-term benefits of their faithfulness.

Solidarity, Suffering, and Calling: Hope For Our Sisters

A team of women from our church illustrate beautifully the power of solidarity with those who suffer. Several years ago, Brooke Sulahian was deeply challenged to enter into the suffering of others in the world after reading Richard Stearns's book *The Hole in Our Gospel* and Nicholas Kristof and Sheryl WuDunn's book *Half the Sky.*

Brooke writes:

God used these challenging books to burst open the "bubble of safety" in which I lived, help me see the world beyond my immediate vision, and allow my heart to break due to the devastating and worldwide oppression of women and girls. While God was doing this painful work in me, I also saw the hope God has placed in the hearts of women and girls and as I learned of their resilience when given the chance to heal, speak, grow, fight back, learn, and contribute. God had invited me to do something for my sisters in need and, gratefully, I said yes.

Brooke began raising awareness and asking others to join in the effort, and they became involved in raising funds for obstetric fistula surgeries to correct the damage done to young women due to previous errant surgeries. By 2012, they made it a goal to raise funding for one hundred corrective surgeries at $450 per surgery through the Fistula Foundation. That same year, Hope for Our Sisters was born.[8]

These women have chosen to enter into the pain of others by raising awareness about women suffering from fistula. They also are using the example of Hope for Our Sisters "to encourage and mobilize women to follow God's calling on their lives as they are invited to give of their time, talents and treasures."

Conclusion

As more followers of Christ respond faithfully to their own suffering and the suffering of others, the church increasingly will be transformed into a fellowship of the suffering. As the church is transformed into a fellowship of the suffering, we increasingly will believe the world has the potential of being transformed by the love of Christ. How can that be? We imagine and pray that if this vision for the church were caught, Christians would become famous for their abilities to suffer faithfully despite the harshest circumstances. Because everyone ultimately suffers, what if Christians were the people the world turned to most when pain came knocking at their doors? What if Christians were the people the hurting could turn to most when they sought not only healing but solidarity and hope? We might taste and see fellowship like we have never experienced before—not merely between other believers but with anyone God places before us.

Suffering comes with the territory because suffering unites us with Christ and with each other like nothing else can.

Forging Fellowship Reflections

1. Why do you think the church in the Western world experiences so little literal persecution? How can we prepare ourselves for the day it might come?

2. Even after seeing people suffering severely in the media or meeting them on short-term mission trips, why is it so easy to forget them? How can we change that in ourselves?

3. In what way can you engage in the suffering of our persecuted Christian family around the world?

Pain as Common Ground

Neighboring Through Suffering

As I took up my life as a minister, I tried to understand why so many people resisted and rejected God. I soon realized that perhaps the main reason was affliction and suffering. . . . But at the same time, I learned that just as many people find God through affliction and suffering.

TIM KELLER, *WALKING WITH GOD THROUGH PAIN AND SUFFERING*

ONE OF THE MOST challenging parts of following Jesus is trying to obey the Bible's commands that appear at first to contradict one another. Take, for instance, what Christians' relationships with their parents should be like. In the Ten Commandments we are explicitly told to "Honor your father and your mother" (Exodus 20:12). Yet in Jesus' teachings, he instructs us, "If anyone comes to me and does not hate father and mother, wife and children, brothers and sisters—yes, even their own life—such a person cannot be my disciple" (Luke 14:26). "Honor your father and mother" and "hate" them? How do we reconcile this? While Jesus is using the exaggerated language of "hate" in this passage to prove his point that nothing or no one—not even one's parents and family—should be a higher priority than him, it still raises the question, What if my efforts to obey Jesus are causing my parents to feel dishonored by me?[1] The Scriptures never state that following Jesus would be easy or simple.

Another tension we commonly hear people express concerns the challenge of trying to obey both Jesus' Second Great Commandment, "Love your neighbor as yourself" (Matthew 22:39), and Jesus' Great Commission, "Go and make disciples of all nations" (Matthew 28:19). While our intentions to share our faith with others may be nothing other than loving, those we share our faith with probably do not always interpret it that way. Thus we must seriously consider: *Are our efforts at evangelism really loving if others do not perceive them as such?* To better feel the weight of this tension, think of the last time someone from another faith or religious sect tried to convince you that their belief system was right or better than yours. How *loved* did you feel in that exchange?

Total confession: When I (Dave) am having a great day with my family or friends, and I see Mormon missionaries approaching me on the street or knocking on doors in the neighborhood, my first reaction is total annoyance. *Can't they just leave us alone!* I think. And then my annoyance typically turns into total avoidance. "Quick, let's cross the street before they make eye contact with us!" "Shut off the lights, and stay away from the windows so they don't know we're here!" Although there are many times when I'm eager to engage in interfaith dialogue, when my day is going well, the last thing I want is to be bothered by someone's attempt to proselytize me.

Our personal experiences of being "evangelized" must cause us to honestly examine if our faith-sharing efforts as Christians are perceived and received any differently. While we'd like to optimistically hope so, we can't be so sure. Thus, if we must share our faith with others as we are commanded by Christ, we must also consider how we can do it in a way that will be received by others more as a loving gift and less as a frustrating interference. This tension is not something we or anyone else can fully resolve, but it is something we must nevertheless enter into.

We'd like to posit a way forward for how the church, as a fellowship of the suffering, can better share our faith, so our actions and words may be best received by others as a real act of love. Our contention is this: *sharing pain earns permission for sharing faith.* Here's what we mean. When we invest our lives deeply enough with our non-Christian family members, friends, coworkers, neighbors, that they feel safe enough to express their pain and hardship with us, often we will be *invited* to share our faith with them. Perhaps this is what the apostle Peter envisioned when he said, "Always be prepared to give an answer to everyone who asks you to give the reason for the hope that you have. But do this with gentleness and respect" (1 Peter 3:15). Let us offer you an example of this dynamic at work.

Recently, we heard the story of a young Christian couple (we'll call them Adam and Lindsey) who had become great friends with another couple who lived down the street (Max and Tara). The two couples often hung out together and became close enough to even take a vacation out West together. While Adam and Lindsey never hid the fact that they were Christians from Max and Tara, they never brought the subject up in any kind of confrontational or awkward way. A year or so into their friendship, Tara's mom suddenly developed cancer and passed away within a few months of her initial diagnosis. Tara and Max were devastated. And so were Adam and Lindsey.

Instead of trying to offer an explanation as to why this happened to Tara's mom, Adam and Lindsey just loved this grieving couple like they would like to be loved if the roles were reversed. They brought flowers and tokens of condolence, and sat mournfully alongside Tara and Max. They dropped off meals and even planned fun outings to try to help Tara and Max take their minds off this sad reality, even if it were only for a couple hours at a time. Then, after a few months, Tara asked Adam and Lindsey if they would pray for her and her family. While this took Adam and Lindsey by surprise, they gladly agreed to do so. Several weeks later, Tara asked Adam about how his faith helped him through some of the tough times he had experienced in life (which he had shared with Max and Tara before). Thus, without having to try to wedge the uncomfortable topic of faith forcefully into a conversation with this grieving couple, Adam and Lindsey's sacrificial love and support, and vulnerability about their own heartache, opened the way for them to be invited to graciously talk about their Christian faith. Because Adam and Lindsey shared their friends' pain, they were invited to share the reasons for the hope they had in Christ. *Sharing pain earns permission for sharing faith.*

We believe this story of Adam and Lindsey's genuine, agenda-free friendship with Max and Tara, and their patient, gentle, and loving response to Tara's loss is a powerful example of how believers can be ready and willing to "make disciples," while doing so in a way that is welcomed. Yes, there undoubtedly are times when Christians must talk about their faith without being explicitly asked. But perhaps pain sharing like this is a different means by which the church, as a fellowship of the suffering, can more lovingly extend the invitation to experience fellowship with Christ to our neighbors both near and far, at home and at work. We believe this approach to *faith sharing through pain bearing* is demonstrated powerfully in the life of Christ and the writings of the apostle Paul.

Jesus' Example of Sharing Faith by Bearing Pain

Before Jesus ever publicly taught a lesson, performed a miracle, or called people to be his disciples, he lived for thirty years (or so) in the same beautiful yet broken, glorious yet suffering-filled world we find ourselves in. He experienced much of the best and the worst it has to offer. Birth and death, plenty and want, rest and recreation, labor and toil, family and friendship, heartache and hope. God the Son immersed himself fully in the entire range of human experience.

Jesus entered this world scandalously—conceived out of wedlock. Growing up in a close-knit, small-town setting, he most certainly would have heard offensive words and received shameful glances, all stemming from the disreputable beginning he couldn't leave behind. Jesus knew what it was like to not belong, to not be the same as everyone else.

His childhood was far from the picture-perfect one we might imagine. In fact, Jesus' earliest days began on the run, as Mary, Joseph, and their newborn son lived as refugees in Egypt, narrowly escaping the death sentence Herod pronounced on the young boys of Bethlehem (Matthew 2:13-18). It's quite likely that as Jesus matured, he learned these stories from his harrowing past. He probably imagined what these boys who were killed would have been like. Would they have been his friends? Or maybe he even questioned why he survived and the others were left to be brutally killed. Pain never distanced itself from Jesus.

Beyond his traumatic beginnings, we can surmise that Jesus would have experienced all the fruitfulness and frustrations we all do as we try and make our way in the world. He learned a trade as a carpenter, which would have inevitably involved mistakes and lots of hard, unforgiving, thankless work. He would have experienced the stress of trying to make ends meet and supporting his relatives amid uncertain circumstances. In fact, Jesus grew up in the context of his people being ruled by an oppressor. Jesus was not governed by elected officials but by Roman force, accompanied by the leadership of corrupt, self-serving Jewish rulers. Injustice was characteristic of Jesus' earthly homeland.

Thus, when Jesus began his public ministry, he announced the good news of the kingdom as one who had been personally and deeply affected by the hardship of this world. He carried the same burdens as his neighbors, and endured the same crises and heartbreaks. He was truly a man of his people, Israel, a nation whose given name means "struggle," which characterized their calling and plight in the world. Out of this family and life of struggle, Jesus announced good news. Out of this pain, Jesus offered himself.

Perhaps the reason Jesus was so widely sought after throughout his ministry was not merely because of his compelling teaching or his miraculous healing powers, but because he understood the people he ministered to so intimately. People felt known by Jesus like they never had before. As the woman at the well said, "Come, see a man who told me everything I ever did" (John 4:29). Who of us can be known apart from our pain? Jesus knew the people he shared the good news with, because Jesus shared their pain.

Quite possibly, the most poignant, explicit example of how faith sharing is born first out of pain bearing is Jesus' interaction with the thief on the cross. As Jesus endures the same, unimaginable capital punishment as these condemned criminals, it becomes clear to one of the two men that Jesus is not like them, or like anyone else for that matter. He is the Messiah. So with some of the last ounces of strength he has, this criminal cries out, "Jesus, remember me when you come into your kingdom." Jesus answers, "Truly I tell you, today you will be with me in paradise" (Luke 23:42-43). Just as Jesus was with this man in his suffering on the cross, so this man will be with Jesus in his glory. In the same way, could it be possible that the more we enter into and share the pain of our neighbors, the more our neighbors may have the opportunity to enter into and share the life of Christ with us?

Comforted to Bring Comfort

Along with Christ's example, Paul's letters also affirm that God's kingdom grows through *faith-sharing through pain-bearing*. This dynamic might be part of what Paul had in mind when he charged the church in Corinth to comfort others with the comfort they had received in Christ. He writes, "Praise be to the God and Father of our Lord Jesus Christ, the Father of compassion and the God of all comfort, who comforts us in all our troubles, so that we can comfort those in any trouble with the comfort we ourselves receive from God" (2 Corinthians 1:3-4). Here we see unfold a critical progression in our life and ministry with God. The invitation we receive when we suffer is fellowship with God. God invites us into fellowship not only so we might receive comfort and healing, but so we might extend that same fellowship to others when they suffer.

What might this extension of fellowship with God look like? First, it entails building solidarity with those who suffer. The Greek word translated as "comfort" in this passage is the word *paraklēsis*, which can be understood as "coming alongside." This meaning of the word is well-captured by *The Message* translation of these verses, "He [God] comes alongside us when we go through hard times, and before you know it, he brings us alongside someone else who is going through hard times so that we can be there for that person just as God was there for us."

Think for a moment of some of the ways God has been there for you in your suffering. God might be putting people on your path who are going through disappointments similar to those you've gone through, so you can offer them what God extended to you. We'll explore how we can be there for others through several examples that follow. But important for us to note for now is that in order to extend fellowship with God with those who are hurting, we must first come alongside them. When come alongside others in their pain, God can work through us to comfort them through his presence embodied in us.

As we begin to extend fellowship with God to others by building solidarity with them, we can, second, continue to extend that fellowship further by sharing the hope found in the truth of who God is. Paul begins this call to the pain-sharing work of ministry by reminding the Corinthians of the character of the God they serve. Paul describes him as "the Father of compassion and the God of all comfort" (2 Corinthians 1:3). We can experience fellowship with God in our pain because he is a compassionate God, one who has suffered like us, with us, and ultimately for us. Only he knows the depths of what we are experiencing, and only in him can the most life-giving, hope-instilling consolation be found. This is why we must never settle to comfort others by merely being there for them. While being there is essential to the ministry of comforting, it's not complete. As opportunities arise, we must patiently and gently comfort people with the truth of who God is. In knowing the character and reality of who God is, we discover a way to keep going despite our most intensely felt pain.

Thus, from both Jesus' example and Paul's teaching, we learn that God does not extend fellowship to us when we suffer so we alone may be comforted, but so we, in turn, may extend his fellowship to others—both inside and outside the church. By helping to bear the pain others carry, we can be given permission—and even an invitation—to share our faith with them as well.

It's not every day, though, that someone asks us to bear their burdens and share their suffering with them. So how might we, as a fellowship of the suffering, share the hardships others experience in such a way that we may one day be given permission to share our faith? While this question defies a one-size-fits all formula, we nevertheless offer several ways to engage with ourselves, God, and

Evangelistic Suffering

Have you ever seen a book on evangelistic suffering? We know plenty of *why* books on suffering and some theological treatises on "how God could let this happen," but nothing on "how to use your suffering for the sake of the kingdom." Perhaps the book is out there, but it certainly has never become a bestseller!

I (Paul) was thinking of this as I sat recently at the diabetic clinic waiting for my quarterly appointment. I thought about how God has used this disease to put me in touch as a witness with all sorts of people who I'd otherwise never have met—from my Jewish doctor, who is fascinated by our missionary travels, to other diabetics struggling with depression as they seek to manage the disease.

The Bible is full of stories of God using suffering for his purposes. Joseph's suffering in Egypt as a slave and then a prisoner was used to save the twelve tribes of Israel. Esther endured hardship and risked her life for the preservation of God's people. Daniel and his three friends suffered at the hands of Babylonian and Medo-Persian kings so they could point these pagans to the one true God. The apostles valued their suffering because it helped them to identify with Jesus and put them (as witnesses) before kings, rulers, and influential leaders.

When we encounter hardship, if God doesn't answer our first prayer (which is *always*, "God, please take away the pain"), then we can pray, "Okay then, Lord, please use the pain for your purposes. Put me into ministry with others who need to know your comfort." For example, "I wish I had a job, but use me this week in the unemployment line." "I pray for a relief of my loneliness, but use me to reach out to people lonelier than me." "I'm praying that you'll heal this cancer, but if you don't, please use me this week at my chemotherapy treatment."

Jesus provides the ultimate example of evangelistic suffering. Though he wanted to be relieved of facing the cross, he nonetheless prayed, "Not my will, but yours, O God. Use my pain. Use my suffering. I release myself— and my suffering—to you."[2]

others in order to learn how our *common human pain* might become the *common ground* on which faith-filled conversations can grow.

Engaging Our Own Suffering

To share effectively in the pain of others, we must start by engaging our own. All too often, rather than dealing with our sufferings head-on, the most common way many of us handle hardship is by *avoiding* it. Avoidance typically takes one of three forms. First, we are tempted to *minimize* our sufferings. We act as if they're nothing. "It's no big deal." *Nothing to worry about*, we tell ourselves. Pain minimizers tend to treat mountain-sized problems as molehill-shaped inconveniences. We naively think they'll simply go away.

Second, many of us gravitate toward avoiding our pain by keeping ourselves perpetually *distracted*. When aching feelings of suffering start to arise in our hearts, we try to soothe ourselves with something else to make these emotions go away. That something else is often extreme television viewing, Internet surfing, or social media browsing. The reason many of us are tempted to binge watch Netflix is not because of its great programming but because it is so displacing. It makes us feel free from the discouragement of our real lives by keeping us perpetually distracted. It's not uncommon for sports to play a similar role. Even worse than "screen soothing" is distracting ourselves through overdrinking, overmedicating, or overindulging in a substance in an attempt to numb our feelings. These things might temporarily take us away from the moment, but they will never permanently take away our pain. Ultimately, they will only make circumstances far worse.

A third way we tend to avoid our pain is by *running away* from it—either literally or by never slowing down. We literally run away from our pain when we leave one place and move to another. Our hunch is that one of the unspoken reasons why we live in such a transient culture is because people are striving to leave behind the hurts they've accumulated in one place, hoping they won't follow them to another. While there are certainly justified instances where moving might be the wisest course of action, all too often we leave a place prematurely because we're simply trying to avoid the deeper issues behind our pain.

Some of us, though, are so adept at running from our suffering that we can do so without physically leaving our present location. All we have to do is load up our schedules to the max so we never have any pauses, downtime, or moments to reflect; thus our pain-filled emotions can't catch up to us. The thinking is, if we never stop moving, we'll never have to feel. As second nature as this strategy might seem, no matter how fast we are, our suffering will ultimately catch us. We can't run from reality forever. It has a way of finding every single one of us.

While many of us have the tendency to avoid our suffering, many others of us respond in the other extreme. We *obsess* over our suffering. If *avoiders* attempt to make our suffering *nothing*, *obsessors* make it *everything*. Obsessors can get so consumed by either "wanting what they don't have" or "having what they don't want" that they completely miss out on enjoying the great things they actually do have. Obsessors are often characterized by bitterness and resentment over the events of their lives. Bitterness over what has likely happened or resentment for what has yet to happen. Or vice versa. For those who haven't gotten what they thought was rightly theirs, entitlement is likely to rise out of the ashes of obsession. "That position. That reward. That lifestyle. That _____ should be mine!" Obsessors likely put everything else in life on hold until they get what they believe they deserve—to their own detriment, and especially to the detriment of others.

Instead of *avoiding* or *obsessing* over our suffering, we offer a third way: *engaging* our suffering. If *avoiders* make suffering *nothing*, and *obsessors* make it *everything*, then *engagers* make it *something*. *Engagers* not only recognize and come to grips with their disappointments, and suffering, but they see the opportunities inherent within them. Namely, the invitation to fellowship.

It wasn't until I was in my mid-twenties that I (Dave) began to engage the suffering I had accrued up to that point in my life. Where I grew up, few people talked about their pain and struggles. If someone was brave enough to do so, they'd likely be looked down on by others. Why? Because expressing emotion was a telltale sign of weakness. Not only so, but talking about *how you're doing* and not just *what you've been doing* could run the risk of making someone feel uncomfortable. So to avoid injecting unnecessary awkwardness into a conversation, the unspoken rule was that you rarely if ever spoke about your inner life. It was just more appropriate not to do so.

The only thing that seemed worse than talking about difficult emotions was actually *feeling* those emotions. For instance, if you were to reveal to someone—say, a parent or close relative—that you were feeling unhappy or depressed, it wouldn't be uncommon for that person to respond by getting upset with *you*: "Hasn't my love been good enough for you?" Or "I knew you have always thought I was a bad parent/sibling/friend/person. This is all my fault!" Instead of receiving the consolation you were hoping for, you might end up having to console the person you spoke to.[3]

Given this cultural milieu, not only did I try to avoid talking about my painful emotions, but up until my mid-to-early twenties I endeavored to avoid them altogether. That was almost totally derailed, though, after I got married to a mental health counseling student!

The best and most frustrating part of marrying Erin is that she has the ability to know what I am feeling before I have any clue that I'm feeling it. When she's asks me what's wrong, I most often genuinely and honestly answer "nothing." In the past, I used to try to defend my answer by *arguing* that *I'm fine* when she'd push back. But now I accept the fact that when she asks this question, I'm probably not fine, I'm just *unengaged*, either consciously or unconsciously, with my inner life. (And one day I aspire to know when I'm not fine before Erin does!)

Because it's never a good idea to try to receive counseling from your spouse, I decided to seek out a spiritual director for guidance. Much to my surprise, wading into my own woundedness with God, through the guidance of a spiritual director, was very transformative and has thus become one of the most life-giving practices for me. Trying to engage the suffering in your life by yourself is next to impossible. You need fellowship. If you're like me, you need to find someone like Kent.

For nearly the past ten years, Kent Groff has been my spiritual director, brother in Christ, and friend who has embodied for me most beautifully what it means to be a part of the fellowship of the suffering. Through meeting with Kent, I have been led prayerfully and painfully into the journey of engaging the suffering continually brewing within my soul. Regularly, during our sessions together, Kent both invites me and gives me permission to grieve over the suffering I had grown accustomed to believing was wrong to feel. These times of entering into my hurt and heartache have ultimately brought me profound freedom. Crying—shockingly—has become a gateway for experiencing acutely felt liberation. Even more than my own tears, the tears Kent has shed, because of the suffering *I* have experienced, have brought me closer than I ever could have imagined to the arms of Christ.

The results of these efforts to engage my suffering have had a profound effect on my ministry and mission as a pastor. More often than not, the people God brings into my life have experienced suffering similarly to how I have. More than the theological answers I can offer, or the counseling techniques I've been trained to implement, what has made the biggest impact in the lives of those God has called me to serve has been my own suffering. Sometimes just knowing someone else has been there is what makes all the difference. In some instances, the growth these people have experienced by engaging their pain has so impressed their long-time friends and family that these people have taken steps to more personally discover what life with God is like.

As you take the brave steps of engaging your personal suffering with a fellow sufferer, don't be surprised when you start to notice how God leads you to enter the lives of those who suffer similarly to you. If you want to know what God has called you to do with your life, it's wise to start by engaging your suffering. Your pain might be the biggest platform God gives you for sharing your faith.

A word of caution: Before moving on, let us offer one major caution to all of us as we come alongside those who are suffering. We have learned from experience that if we attempt to comfort others when they suffer, but we haven't first spent enough time and energy engaging our own pain, we become far more likely to act like Job's friends to someone by attempting to explain away someone's pain through clichéd statements and pat answers. If we haven't engaged our own suffering deeply, the suffering of others is likely to make us uncomfortable. And when we feel uncomfortable, we become more likely to say something we might not intend, perhaps in an insensitive way, instead of wisely choosing to remain silent and present. We will all become better pain sharers as we engage our own suffering with God and trusted members of his fellowship.

Engaging the Suffering of Others

As we commit to continually engaging our personal suffering—which is a lifelong process—we become best prepared to engage the suffering of our neighbors. Because every person is different and has their own unique story of suffering, every person should be engaged in a personal way, not through a one-size-fits-all formula. Thus, to engage with others' suffering lovingly and wisely, we must approach others with gentleness, sensitivity, patience, and steadfastness. Moreover, we must be attentive to the tender stirrings of the Holy Spirit, who will always be our most trusted guide as we seek to come alongside our hurting neighbors. Keeping all these indispensable postures of sharing pain in mind, we offer the following as ways to best engage the suffering of those around us.

- *Slow down.* Ratchet back your pace of life enough to have unhurried opportunities to say more than just hello to your neighbors and coworkers.

- *Pay attention.* Often our body language says more about us than our words do. Be fully present to those you interact with so you might notice those who are in need.

- *Be vulnerable.* When someone asks you how you're doing, be open to sharing both a *joy* and a *struggle* you're experiencing. As you become *appropriately vulnerable* about your struggles to others, they may feel safe and comfortable to open up more of what's going on in their lives.

- *Be responsive.* When someone in your office or school goes through a crisis situation in life (which everyone does, of course), be as wisely responsive as you can. Start by trying to meet whatever immediate needs this person might have. Almost always, hurting people need the presence of other people. So come alongside them when they hurt, just as Christ came alongside you. But don't merely do this immediately after a crisis has occurred. Instead, be a steady presence that a hurting person can count on long after the crisis occurred.

▨ *Befriend.* No one wants to be someone else's project. Come alongside others, and let them come alongside you. Some of the most significant friendships are forged out of mutually shared pain. Let yourself be loved in order to love.

▨ *Share good news.* Ultimately, if we are to share the pain of others most fully, we must be able to gently and lovingly share the reason for the hope we have. One of the best ways we can do this is by leading the conversation with your personal experience. How has God met you and comforted you when you've suffered? How has the gospel been good news to you in your pain? And in turn, how might it be good news for this person *now*? Be prepared to share why you have the hope and the joy that you do.

The Platform of Pain

A few summers ago, Jack, one of the men that swam with us at the indoor pool in our community, approached me (Paul) with an unusual question. We were all part of a little group we called the Noon Platoon because we swam laps during our lunch breaks. Jack asked, "Are you going to be in town for the next few weeks? My mother's dying, and you're the only religious person I know. Would you do her funeral?" I agreed immediately.

Jack had been our Noon Platoon colleague for over a decade. He knew about the deaths of three of our four parents, had attended the services after Christie's father and forty-seven-year-old brother died within seven weeks of each other, and he had heard me preach at their funerals. As far as we knew, Christie's father's and brother's funerals were the only time Jack had ever been to any church, but Jack knew that we knew something about loss. Jack had shared in our pain, and now he was inviting us to share in his.

After agreeing to preach, I found myself thinking, *What have you done? You never knew his mother, and to your knowledge she has no faith of any kind—just like Jack.* I secretly hoped that her health and life would linger and that Jack would eventually forget his request.

But about eight days later Jack's mother died. Christie and I stayed with our friend for the wake, the funeral, the graveside service, and the family gathering after the services. At the funeral, I preached a sermon titled "Why Are We Here?" I explained that we were here to remember the deceased, and I delivered her eulogy. Then I observed that we were here to comfort the family in their loss.

And then I said, "Why are we here? The third reason is to ask the question, Why are we here?—not at this funeral, specifically, but on this planet. We confront death, and it forces us to ask the meaning of life. Why indeed *are* we here?" I went on to explain what God says the meaning of life is as explained in the Scriptures, and I gave an overview of his invitation to a relationship with him—now and forever.

I didn't give an invitation; funerals are not a time to exploit peoples' sorrow. I didn't make any official eternal diagnoses about the deceased (other than to release her to God's mercy). I only wanted to confront my listeners with the realities of death in hopes of launching them on a spiritual search.

And the Noon Platoon would hear this gospel message one more time—when the funeral director called me and asked me to preach Jack's funeral a few years later. All of this happened because in our friendship building with Jack, we had openly invited him into our pain and losses. From the platform of sorrow we earned the right to share our faith.

Conclusion

As we have demonstrated, sharing the pain of others can win us great opportunities for sharing faith. Thus, forging fellowship with those who suffer may be one of the most powerful ways we can make disciples in our day and age.

Suffering comes with the territory because it provides unexpected opportunities to love our neighbors and share our faith.

Forging Fellowship Reflections

1. Reread 2 Corinthians 1:4. Are there any painful contexts that God allows you into on a regular basis—AA or other addictive-behavior support meetings, going for chemotherapy (or accompanying a loved one), grief support group, the unemployment office, or painful emotions that you carry inside? How can you pray for God to use you in these contexts?

2. List a few neighbors, coworkers, or family members who (as far as you can tell) have no relationship with God through Jesus Christ. How can you deepen your friendship so that you better love them—even to the point of shared pain?

3. In the list of ways of engaging suffering (see "Engaging the Suffering of Others"), which do you think you will find most difficult and why?

PART FOUR

fellowship
with the
world

The Seed Must Die to Multiply

Mission Through Suffering

The blood of the martyrs is the seed of the Church.

TERTULLIAN, *APOLOGETICUS*

OVER THE SEVERAL DECADES when I (Paul) taught the introductory missions classes at Gordon College, I used Ruth Tucker's book *From Jerusalem to Irian Jaya* as a primary text. Her book provides a historical overview of some of the key people and movements in the more than two-thousand-year history of Christian advancement in the world. Several years ago I realized that though I required the book, it had been a long time since I had actually reread it. So while on vacation, before the next semester began, I decided to read the five-hundred-plus-page book straight through. I read it in two days.

After I completed my reading, Christie asked, "So, what did you learn?"

I responded immediately, "Lots of people died! And those that did not die suffered greatly."

From the martyrs in the book of Acts to Christians burned alive in Nero's garden, from imprisonments to exile to persecutions and violent deaths, our Christian history is full of suffering. Like the twofold tension in Colossians 1, the gospel has indeed gone forward all over the world (Colossians 1:6), but many heralds of the gospel have suffered greatly as they made up "what is still lacking in regard to Christ's afflictions" (Colossians 1:24).

Although our first instinct is to run in the face of opposition or hardship and especially death, our Christian history shows that suffering is the vehicle God often uses to further the reach of his church in global mission. Remember, John Stott said, "The place of suffering in service and of passion in mission is hardly ever taught today. But the greatest single secret of evangelistic or missionary effectiveness is the willingness to suffer and die."[1] We shouldn't be surprised at this. Jesus taught that for a seed to bear fruit, it had to fall into the earth and die (John 12:23-26).

Biblical Framework

If the words of Jesus in John 12:24 stood alone, we could relegate them to some sort of isolated reference to Jesus' imminent death on the cross. Perhaps he was referring to something that would be true of him but not of his followers. But even a casual reading through the New Testament reveals quite the contrary. If we want to come after Jesus, taking up the cross of suffering and hardship is part of the program (Luke 9:23).

Jesus not only observed that he would suffer to fulfill his mission; he also told his disciples that they would follow in his footsteps.

- If they persecuted me, they will also persecute you (John 15:18).

- You won't have a place to lay your head (Matthew 8:20; Luke 9:58).

- You'll be blessed because you tolerate being rejected, maligned, persecuted (Matthew 5:11-12).

- And when hardship comes, bless your oppressors and pray for them (Matthew 5:43-44).

The story continues into the foundations of the church in the book of Acts. Though the book begins with frightened disciples hiding and praying, the empowering presence of the Holy Spirit launches courage in the face of persecution and boldness in the face of threats. The dynamite power of the Holy Spirit transforms them from hibernating cowards to bold witnesses.[2]

Even the religious leaders see the imprint of Jesus in the boldness of his followers (Acts 4:13). Stephen is stoned to death as the persecution spreads, but his testimony plants the seed of the gospel, which helps turn the violent persecutor Saul into the great evangelist and apostle Paul (Acts 7). We often celebrate the story of Peter's miraculous deliverance from prison in Acts 12, but we overlook the fact that James, the brother of John, had been killed only a few verses earlier (Acts 12:2).

Saul of Tarsus gets converted, but Ananias delivers the message with God's promise: "I will show him how much he must suffer for my name" (Acts 9:16). Peter writes letters to comfort and encourage those under great persecution, and the New Testament concludes with a vision of worshiping martyrs at the throne of God (Revelation 7:9-14).

Not too long ago we came across an encouraging booklet titled *The Pocket Promise Book*. It had a myriad of God's beautiful promises recorded in the Bible—promises of forgiveness, of God's guiding presence, of God's peace in the storms of life. They were all encouraging and comfort oriented, which is probably why the booklet didn't include the promise Paul recorded in 2 Timothy. As Paul faces his own imminent death, he reminds Timothy and the believers at Timothy's church in Ephesus, "In fact, everyone who wants to live a godly life in Christ Jesus will be persecuted" (2 Timothy 3:12).

We might not want to claim that promise, but it reaffirms a biblical truth that has played out in our Christian history.

Historical Framework

Jesus' statement of the dying seed bringing forth fruit has been part of our Christian history throughout the ages. The foundation laid by the lives of those who went as missionary pioneers often included physical, emotional, relational, and spiritual suffering. But their suffering provoked the spread of the gospel.

At a mission conference in Accra, Ghana, over four hundred university students came together to hear the challenge to give their lives to taking the gospel message in word and deed to the ends of the earth—especially to the tough places where Jesus had never been preached. The first four speakers—all Ghanaians—told the stories of the British missionaries who had first brought the gospel to Ghana in the mid-nineteenth century.

They reminded these students that their faith was a result of people coming who literally died to bring their forefathers and foremothers the gospel message. They told of these young adults who set sail from England, having packed their earthly belongings in their own caskets because they knew that they would most likely never return from West Africa. An estimated 60 percent of these servants of Christ died in their first two years of service. One church along the Gold Coast of Ghana has buried under the pulpit the missionaries who planted the church; they came at age twenty-six and died at age twenty-eight. In another location, a graveyard bears the headstones of the children of missionaries who died as their parents served: most of the children were younger than ten.

The speakers then reminded these students that Ghana was now a missionary-sending country—with thousands of Ghanaians taking the gospel to others—in the same way as others had brought it to them. The speakers then asked, "Will you enter the fellowship of those willing to suffer that others might know the message of salvation?"

This question pushed me back into my own college years when I chose to say yes to that question. As I listened to these Ghanaian speakers, I realized the impact on my own worldview from the biography of Jim Elliot (see chap. 1). Jim's death, combined with his most quoted phrase, "He is no fool who gives up what he cannot keep to gain what he cannot lose," had shaped my life. Choosing to enter that fellowship has taken Christie and me (Paul) out to encourage believers serving in the most difficult places: wartime visits to Sri Lanka, Angola, Mozambique, and Lebanon; refugee camps in Pakistan and Afghanistan; dangerous places in Colombia, Nigeria, and inner-city United States.

When we read the compendium of Christian suffering in books such as *The New Foxe's Book of Martyrs, Redeemed by Fire* (about the church in twentieth-century China), or *By Their Blood: Christian Martyrs of the Twentieth Century*, we discover that our comfortable Christianity in the Western world has been more the historical exception rather than the norm.[3]

An experience in the Bible study group that Christie and I attend revealed our disconnectedness to our own Christian history. I was soon departing on a teaching/speaking trip to Nigeria and requested prayer concerning a variety of dangers (tough land travel, religious violence, etc.). I knew this journey would take me on tough roads in a location where bandits were common, police were often corrupt, and the extremist group Boko Haram had a presence.

One of the group members sweetly replied, "Remember, the safest place to be is in the center of God's will."

I thought before responding. I thought of the five young men killed by the Aucas tribesmen in 1956; before they departed, they were sent off singing, "We rest on Thee, our shield and our defender." They expected fruitfulness; they got speared to death. I thought of those British missionaries who came to Ghana and West Africa with their earthly belongings packed in their own coffins. I remembered the first missionaries to Sri Lanka who Ajith Fernando describes in his book *The Call to Joy and Pain*. He describes the pioneer visionary from Great Britain who died on the journey, another who died after eight months of service, and eight others who died before they were thirty.[4] I thought of the movie *The Passion of the Christ* and the brutal suffering and death Jesus endured. I thought to myself, *Surely these people were in the center of God's will— especially Jesus! And their lives were anything but safe.*

I thanked the Bible study member for the good words of encouragement, but I went on: "I love that phrase. I've heard it since I was a child. *It's not true,* but it's romantically comforting."

Our Bible study member reacted quite angrily. "Oh, no!" she exclaimed. "It's true: the safest place to be is in the center of God's will."

I realized that I had burst her comfortable Western bubble, which wants safety and security over faith and obedience. I tried one more time to explain: "The center of God's will is the *right* place to be, but it's not necessarily the safest place. Our Lord Jesus and our Christian history bear it out."

Before offering some personal observations about suffering and mission, a brief reality check. We do not want to romanticize suffering. As the missionaries packed their own coffins with their earthly belongings, nobody was laughing. Nor do we want to encourage anyone to seek suffering—as if it guarantees missionary success. Tertullian's famous quotation, that "the blood of the martyrs is the seed of the Church," illustrates a powerful reality in Christian history, but it is not true 100 percent of the time. Suffering has at times crushed the church and at other times led to missionaries (or the children of those missionaries) abandoning their faith.

Because we are personally afraid of suffering and things like beatings, robbery, torture, and violent death, we always appreciate servants of Christ who honestly report on the fears they face as they serve in dangerous contexts. One servant of Christ in Lebanon told the story of building relationships with members of the terrorist group Hezbollah. As a result, he and a colleague were invited to come to the eastern part of the country to talk with the leaders of that group—presumably to explain their Christian faith. Though they were delighted for the invitation, they were also realistic. As they were on their way to speak with and present Jesus to these members of Hezbollah, they realized that they might be riding into their death (or something worse—like brutal torture and eventual slow beheading).

They went. But (and this is where the reality of our humanness comes into play) our Lebanese friend reported that they would stop periodically along the way to vomit. Steps of faith. Stop and vomit. More steps of faith. Stop for more vomiting. You get the picture. We love the human reality in this story because it reminds us that faith is not fearlessness but rather courage in the face of fear. The psalmist didn't write, "Because I have faith, I am never afraid." Instead, he spoke honestly: *"When* I am afraid, I put my trust in you" (Psalm 56:3).

If we live in peaceful places that honor human rights and freedom of religion, thank God. But let's not make our life choices based on perceived safety but rather on the call of God (see chap. 10). And let's never forget those who do suffer in ways we might never imagine (see chap. 7).

Personal Framework

How can we understand the suffering that may come to us as we engage in the local and global mission of God? How might we prepare for the sacrifices and subsequent losses God might call us to?

On a personal level, how can we learn to carry our daily crosses and make the choice to endure some form of hardship so someone else might benefit? Elisabeth Elliot writes,

> We are not often called to great sacrifice, but daily we are presented with the chance to make small ones—a chance to make someone cheerful, a chance to do some small thing to make someone else comfortable or contented, a chance to lay down our petty preferences or cherished plans. This probably requires us to relinquish something—our own convenience or comfort, our own free evening, our warm fireside, or even our habitual shyness or reserve or pride.[5]

When confronting suffering of any degree, small or large, consider four observations that we have made.

First, the best way to prepare for hardship or suffering is personal discipline—before suffering comes. When we think of discipline, we refer to it as "chosen suffering." Watch military personnel as they train for battle or Olympian or Paralympian athletes as they prepare for competition (some overcoming great physical limitations). You can hear the grunting and panting; you can see their sweat and exhaustion. They are preparing themselves in advance for the battles or games or races to come.

Spiritual disciplines are challenges, discomforts, or hardships we choose so we might be equipped for the day when difficulties come. Fasting prepares us for the possibility of living with deprivations. Refraining from weight gain and maintaining healthy exercise disciplines prepare us to have energy during the tougher times of life. Memorizing Scripture prepares us for the possibility of being in contexts where we don't have access to a Bible. Bearing witness to Jesus in peaceful times helps us be ready for bold witness in difficult times. Choosing a simple lifestyle prepares us for some of the inconveniences we might encounter serving alongside brothers and sisters in other parts of the world.

This "chosen suffering" idea lies behind Paul's words to Timothy as he compares the Christian life to that of soldiers in active service, athletes competing to win, and hardworking farmers working for an abundant crop (2 Timothy 2:1-7). Paul also alludes to the Christian life as winning a race or entering a boxing match. Instead of running aimlessly or simply shadowboxing, he lives a life of discipline— "beating my body and making it my slave" (1 Corinthians 9:27).

Second, today's suffering may be preparing us for tomorrow's mission, tomorrow's fruitfulness. Jewel Hyun is a distinguished Korean American woman from our church. In the past decade or more, she has developed a love for and investment in Kenya. More specifically, she is passionate about training and equipping women and girls in Kenya. Because of my (Paul) books and crosscultural experience, Jewel adopted me as her missionary mentor. We would meet over coffee and talk about things such as worldview, crosscultural sensitivity, and relationship building.

On one occasion, Jewel came with a specific question. She was supposed to speak to a Kenyan woman's conference. Many of the women attending were from agrarian backgrounds and some were marginally literate. Jewel asked, "How do I start? How do I connect with these women?"

I understood the question. In general, Jewel lives a moderate middle-class American life in suburban Boston, and drives a nice car. She is a meticulous dresser, and I've never seen her with a single hair out of place. The question about connecting with Kenyan women who work the fields and live in basic housing was a good one. From appearance, you'd assume that these women were worlds apart from Jewel.

"Start by telling the women your story," I suggested.

"My testimony?" she asked.

"No," I said. Jewel had shared her own story with me, so I suggested, "Tell them your testimony of being a refugee as you and your family escaped North Korea. Tell them about being homeless, about being afraid, about being destitute. If the women look at you now, they will think you understand nothing of their world and their experiences. But tell them your background, and they will think, *she knows.*"

One of themes of this book is that God wants to redeem our suffering, our hardships, and our unexplained, unanswered prayers. In Jewel's case, her childhood misery was now the bridge to these women.

Over the past decade we have been at a variety of student missions conferences like the one in Ghana. Four of these gatherings stand out because they took place in countries that experienced extreme Christian persecution in the mid to late twentieth century. In Cuba, over three hundred youth and young adults gathered to hear God's call to missions. In Uganda and Ethiopia, several hundred university students listened to the biblical mandate to go to all nations. In Nepal, over seven hundred new Christians (most from Hindu backgrounds) gathered to study the Scriptures.

The most striking feature at these conferences was not the students but the male and female conference organizers, standing in the back of the room. Most were fifty to seventy years old, and all of them had suffered greatly in their earlier decades. The older Cuban leaders had survived Castro's reeducation (brain-washing) camps in the 1960s. The older Uganda and Ethiopian leaders had stayed faithful (even after seeing colleagues die) under the tyranny of the dictators Idi Amin and Mengistu Haile Mariam in the 1980s. And the older Nepali saints had spent years in prison for converting and then evangelizing others when both actions were illegal in pre-1991 Nepal.

How do we process the internal or external suffering that we might be experiencing? We learn from others that God is doing something we don't understand and preparing us for later impact.

Pain Is Part of the Plan
by Evan Burns

I grew up with a health disability that would have prevented me from going to college, obtaining a job, or living a long, normal life. Before God mercifully delivered me from it, he graciously delivered me through it. Many days and nights I lay in the darkness of my room in much pain and nausea, praying in the silence that God would give me the sustaining grace to preach the gospel to the nations. I started preseminary at the age of five when God sent me my wisest and most influential teacher: affliction. Through his loving discipline, God taught me about his sovereign goodness and inscrutable wisdom.

Having grown up facing much affliction, and having learned well the theology of suffering under a sovereign God, I was still naive to how unrelenting and inexplicable the trials of the missionary life are. If not for the doctrine of God's wise sovereignty in suffering, I would never have made it. Long-term missions can indeed be a place of excitement and adventure; however, it is also inescapably a place of adversity and barrenness. It is moreover the land of self-emptying and learning to laugh at yourself; learning to think, feel, dream, and

reason in a foreign language; learning to enjoy the adopted family of Christ in light of distant relationships back home; learning to keep silent in the face of stiff criticism from those who once supported you; learning to eat the Word of God as your daily food; learning to pray for your wife and children because their lives literally depend on it; and learning to navigate wisely on the path of self-denial amid a global culture immersed in self-indulgence, self-promotion, and self-preservation.

I would soberly admonish any missionary candidate that the mission field is not all romance and radical adventure; it is also mingled with heartbreak, loss, and self-denial. But therein we discover God's boundless love and wise providence. C. S. Lewis said in his poem *As the Ruin Falls*, "The pains you give me are more precious than all other gains."

Perhaps D. A. Carson says it best in his excellent book on suffering, *How Long, O Lord? Reflections on Suffering and Evil*: "The more the leaders are afflicted with weakness, suffering, perplexity, and persecution, the more it is evident that their vitality is nothing other than the life of Jesus. This has enormously positive spiritual effects on the rest of the church. The leaders' death means the church's life. This is why the best Christian leadership cannot simply be appointed. It is forged by God himself in the fires of suffering, taught in the school of tears. There are no shortcuts."

God loves his servants so much that he allows them to suffer, so that his grace will sustain them in order to make his glory known. Our weakness is the God-ordained instrument through which the Holy Spirit fills us with the power of Christ.

Evan Burns and his wife, Kristie, have served as long-term missionaries in the Middle East, East Asia, and now in Southeast Asia. He also serves as assistant professor of spirituality and missiology and director of online education at Asia Biblical Theological Seminary in Thailand.[6]

Third, suffering at the hands of others or by the actions of others will take us into a deeper understanding of forgiveness. We frequently refer to Paul the apostle as the greatest evangelist of the early years of church growth, but we might argue that "greatest" should be reserved for Stephen in Acts 7. His testimony of forgiveness—as he was being stoned to death under the supervision of Saul of Tarsus!—planted the gospel message of forgiveness in Saul's head.

As Stephen is dying, he remembers the words of Jesus on the cross and personalizes them to his persecutors. Jesus' "Father forgive them" on the cross becomes Stephen's "Do not hold this against them."

Throughout Christian history, many servants of Christ have been strengthened by the realization that in some mysterious way, they are participating in the ongoing sufferings of Christ. The apostles rejoiced that they had been considered worthy to suffer shame for Jesus' name (Acts 5:41). Paul wrote about making up what is lacking in the sufferings of Christ (Colossians 1:24), and he defined the scars of his beatings as the brand marks of Jesus (Galatians 6:17).

Understanding that we live under the sign of the cross helps us see both the sacrifice of our Lord and his grace in forgiving his persecutors. It is that same grace that enabled Gladys Staines to forgive the religious extremists in Orissa state, India, who brutally burned to death her husband and two young sons. It is that same grace that enabled Lalani Jayasinghe to forgive (and later serve) the religious extremists who shot and killed her husband in southern Sri Lanka.

Helen Roseveare served many years in the country we now know as the Democratic Republic of Congo. At the Urbana 76 student missions conference, she told the story of surviving the brutal rape and enslavement by the Simba rebels during their struggle for independence in 1964. But as she reflected back on the experience, her dominant theme was privilege:

> One word became unbelievably clear, and that word was privilege. He didn't take away pain or cruelty or humiliation. No! It was all there, but now it was altogether different. It was with him, for him, in him. He was actually offering me the inestimable privilege of sharing in some little way the edge of the fellowship of his suffering.
>
> In the weeks of imprisonment that followed and in the subsequent years of continued service, looking back, one has tried to "count the cost," but I find it all swallowed up in privilege. The cost suddenly seems very small and transient in the greatness and permanence of the privilege.[7]

Fourth, our endurance or grace under pressure, hardship, or suffering becomes our witness. In a *Christianity Today* article titled "Outpacing Persecution," the author reports on the amazing growth of the church in India in the face of intensifying persecution from a radical Hindu movement called "Hindutva." Vivian Fernandes, a Baptist leader in Mumbai, summarized the situation in biblical, historical terms: "Like the early church in Acts, persecution helps the church to grow spiritually and expand." Paul Cornelius from the Asia Theological Association takes it a step further: "The right prayer is not for persecution to go away but for sustenance through it."[8]

Christie and I (Paul) visited John and Nancy at their home in Beirut, Lebanon, toward the end of that country's more than twenty-year civil war. We heard numerous stories of surviving multiple bombings while cradling their children in their arms as they huddled in the stairwell of the apartment building. They brought out boxes of shrapnel that they had collected over the years.

John is a Lebanese citizen, but because Nancy had an American passport, they were free throughout the war to leave Lebanon. When we asked local Christians about John and Nancy's ministry, almost every person replied with the same two words: *"They stayed."* Their willingness to endure hardship with others became their greatest witness to their love for Jesus, their love for their people, and their love for their country. They stayed.

On a visit to Beijing, China, our colleague Stephanie, an English teacher, took us to church with four of her students who had come to faith. The preacher that Sunday was an old man—easily eighty-plus years. He was soft-spoken, stooped over, and walked slowly to the pulpit. His sermon was in Mandarin, so we didn't understand a word, but my impression was that his sermon was pretty low energy, even boring.

We went out with Stephanie and the four young men for lunch, and I asked them about the service. I specifically asked, "The old man who preached—was he a good preacher?" The four young men responded, "Oh yes!" And one of them went on. "He is a great preacher. He spent many years in prison for Jesus."

Their measurement was neither charisma nor volume, not relevance or intellectual prowess. They looked at his life of perseverance in the face of prison and suffering. The shadow of the cross in his life overshadowed all other measurements. In *The Cross of Christ*, John Stott captures it this way:

> It is the crucified man that can preach the cross. Said Thomas "except I shall see in his hands the print of the nails . . . I will not believe." Dr. Parker of London said that what Thomas said of Christ, the world is saying about the church. And the world is also saying to every preacher: Unless I see in your hands the print of the nails, I will not believe. It is true. It is the man . . . who has died with Christ . . . that can preach the cross of Christ.[9]

Suffering and Success Go Together

Like it or not, mission and suffering are part of our story. But sometimes, when we find ourselves in the midst of the story, we aren't able to anticipate what God might do through our hardships. In those times it's good to remember those who have gone before us.

Though none of us are likely to pass through intense suffering, consider what is arguably one of the greatest mission-and-suffering stories of Christian history. To start, join Christie and me (Paul) briefly on a ministry trip to Burma (Myanmar) several years ago. Under the auspices of the World Evangelical Alliance and the Myanmar Evangelical Fellowship, we traveled to Yangon, Myanmar (Rangoon, Burma), to speak to youth and youth workers.

To connect our trip with missions history, we decided to re-read the biography of Adoniram Judson, pioneer to Burma, during our trip. Judson and his wife, Nancy (also called Ann) Hasseltine Judson, went out as one of the first North American missionaries, sailing in 1812 from Salem, Massachusetts.[10]

When we arrived, the Burmese capital city, still dominated by the overwhelming Shwedagon Pagoda, looked much like the city

Judson described to supporters at home. With the exception of signs of technological development and the increased population, we could easily imagine the Judsons sailing up the Irrawaddy River facing unknown challenges and what we know now as unimaginable hardship.

Indeed, the most striking aspect of the Judson Burma story is endurance in spite of suffering. From start to finish, his biography describes hardship. He, his family, and his coworkers experienced affliction almost unparalleled in modern mission history.

Lest we forget, however, Judson pursued his calling knowing full well that sufferings lay ahead—a significant lesson in itself to us Christians two hundred years later, whose first question is often, "Is it safe to go there?"

In writing to Ann Hazeltine's father for permission to marry her, Judson wrote:

I have now to ask whether you can consent to part with your daughter early next spring, to see her no more in this world. Whether you can consent to see her departure to a heathen land, and her subjection to the hardships and sufferings of a missionary life? Whether you can consent to her exposure to the dangers of the ocean; to the fatal influence of the southern climate of India; to every kind of want and distress; to degradation, insult, persecution, and perhaps a violent death? Can you consent to all this, for the sake of perishing immortal souls; for the sake of Zion and the glory of God? Can you consent to all this, in hope of soon meeting your daughter in the world of glory, with a crown of righteousness brightened by the acclamations of praise which shall redound to her Savior from heathens saved, through her means, from eternal woe and despair?[11]

His anticipation of the hardships ahead almost all came true. Their tribulations began on their voyage to India (his first anticipated destination) from Salem, Massachusetts. A devout Congregationalist, Judson had not resolved the issue of baptism by immersion, so he set his sights on studying the issue on the three-month sail. On the journey, he decided that the Baptist perspective was the correct one, and he and Nancy were baptized upon arrival. He wrote to his Congregationalist supporters in Massachusetts, provoking the first crisis. They immediately cut all of their support.

Support from Baptists came, but not without some very uncomfortable weeks. But this problem was only the beginning. The Judsons encountered visa difficulties in India, and their first years took them from India to Mauritius (Isle of France) to Malaysia, while considering both Ceylon (now Sri Lanka) and Java (part of Indonesia). They reluctantly ended up in Burma in 1813. Anguish and struggles in Burma included

- more than two years to learn Burmese, in a country where no English was spoken;

- six years to the first Christian convert, Maung Nau, in 1819;

- torture of young Burmese Christians by the government in 1819;

- suspicion of being a spy during civil war with Britain, followed by a torturous stint in the "Death Prison" (1824–1825), which included being hung every night upside down in leg-irons as well as a "death march" that nearly killed him;

- a temporary loss of his accumulated translation work in 1824 (eventually recovered);

- severe depression (what we would call clinical depression, verging on insanity) in 1828 that followed Nancy's death;

- falling away of new Burmese believers; and

■ a lifetime devoted to one primary task: to give the Burmese a Bible in their own language.

As hard as it is to believe, these struggles pale in comparison to the amount of personal grief that surrounded the Judson mission. Reviewing the detailed account of Judson's life in *To the Golden Shore* illustrates the biblical teaching that "unless a kernel of wheat falls to the ground and dies, it remains only a single seed. But if it dies, it produces many seeds" (John 12:24).[12]

Statistics are not clear, but it seems that there were between a dozen and twenty-five enduring Burmese converts at the time of Judson's death. No matter what the statistics, the Judson mission deaths seem to have equaled or exceeded the number of converts.

But one mission had been completed. The Burmese had the Bible in their own language—with a Burmese-English dictionary completed as well.

Leave the Judson saga and return with my wife and me to our visit a few years ago. In a meeting with youth and youth leaders, we picked up a copy of the Burmese Bible. The Burmese script was unreadable for us, but we noticed one English sentence on the title page: "Translated by the Reverend A. Judson."

A Bible translation that had stood the test of time—over 150 years! It stands as a testimony to Judson's scholarship and meticulous linguistic study.

I took the Bible over to our host, the head of the Evangelical Fellowship. "Matthew," I asked, pointing to the English sentence, "Do you know who this man is—Judson?"

"Oh yes!" he exclaimed. "Whenever someone mentions the name Judson great tears come to our eyes because we know what he and his family suffered for us."

**Chronology of
Adoniram Judson's Loss**

• 1812. The Judsons and the Newells set sail to India.

• 1813. Harriet Newell and her child die at sea, en route to Mauritius.

• 1814. A European woman employed in Mauritius by the Judsons dies.

• 1814. Nancy gives birth to a stillborn child at sea, en route to Burma.

• 1814. Potential coworker Felix Carey departs Burma, sailing up the Irrawaddy River; the boat capsizes, and Felix's wife and two children die.

• 1816. The Judson's first son, Roger Williams Judson, dies in his second year of life.

• 1819. Coworker Edward Wheelock dies.

• 1821. Mr. Newell (husband of Harriet) dies in Bombay.

• 1826. Judson's beloved partner and true soul mate, Nancy, dies in October.

• 1826. Mrs. Price, wife of medical coworker Dr. Price, dies three days after Nancy.

• 1826. Mr. Rodgers and Mr. Hall, Christian friends in Burma, die— Rodgers as a result of the Death Prison.

• 1827. Dr. Price dies.

• 1827. Less than six months after Nancy's death, their baby Maria dies at two years, three months, on April 24.

• 1830. Judson Wade Boardman, son of George Boardman, who had been recruited as a church planter in the north, dies.

• 1831. George Boardman dies and leaves his young wife, Sarah, and the rest of their family alone, north of Rangoon.

• 1834. Judson marries Sarah Boardman, widow of George.

• 1836. Luther Rice, a friend and supporter in Burma, dies.

• 1841. Sarah gives birth to a stillborn son, Luther Judson.

• 1841. Henry Judson dies at age one year, seven months.

• 1845. Sarah Boardman Judson dies.

• 1845. Charlie Judson dies, age one year, six months.

• 1848. Judson travels to the United States, meets and marries his third wife, Emily.

• 1850. After completing his translation and the Burmese-English dictionary, Judson sails into the Indian Ocean in hopes of clearing his lungs from ongoing tuberculosis. He dies at sea and is buried in obscurity.

• 1850. Charles Judson, son of Adoniram and Emily Judson, dies at birth on April 22.

• 1854. Emily Judson dies of tuberculosis on June 1.

He went on with great emotion, "We know about the sicknesses they endured. We read about the death march and the death prison. We know about the wives who died, and the children who died, and the coworkers who died.

"But today, there are over two million Christians in Myanmar, and every one of us traces our spiritual heritage to one man—the Reverend Adoniram Judson."

Later in the nineteenth century, one of Adoniram's only surviving sons, Edward, speaking at the dedication of the Judson Memorial Church in New York City, summarized his father's story: "Suffering and success go together. If you are succeeding without suffering, it is because others before you have suffered; if you are suffering without succeeding, it is that others after you may succeed."

Judson probably illustrated this truth as much as any man who ever lived. He and his family were truly grains that fell to the earth and died so that they could bear fruit. Probably the greatest lesson we can learn from the life of this devout man is that we have to trust in the work of God, even if our efforts seem fruitless and wasted. Judson's life is proof that God is faithful in bringing about his work in due time, and we simply need to remain faithful and trusting in him.

When Adoniram Judson died on April 11, 1850, he had not seen vast numbers saved directly through his ministry. He will be remembered, however, for his role in the establishment of US missions, his outstanding translation of the Bible into Burmese, and his foundational work among the Burmese people.

Conclusion

In God's kingdom-building work, success is virtually impossible apart from suffering. Whenever, wherever, and however God calls us, we must prepare to endure the rough roads and tough terrains that our ancestors before us trod. There's simply no way around pain on the narrow road.

Suffering comes with the territory because suffering advances God's mission to the ends of the earth.

Forging Fellowship Reflections

1. Following Jesus to the ends of the earth (or to the end of the street, for that matter) will involve risks and potential suffering. It might not be "safe." But how do we distinguish taking risks of faith from doing things out of foolish presumptuousness?

2. The life of Adoniram Judson (or other missionary martyrs) can often cause feelings of guilt and disconnectedness—"I have never suffered like *that!*" But taken down to daily life, what practical observations in these lives can help us deal with daily hardships?

3. Read Hebrews 12:1-3. What does the author offer us so that we do not get discouraged or distracted by suffering as we engage in God's global mission?

Are You Really Passionate?

Calling Through Suffering

*And if I miss that Christianity is about passionate, suffering love,
I've missed its essence.*

ANN VOSKAMP, *THE BROKEN WAY*

GROWING THROUGH SUFFERING, staying faithful in the face
of hardship, and enduring losses of various types is never easy.
The pain stays with us. The long-term battle with chronic diseases
wears us down. We ask God *why* and then sit uncomfortably in
silence. We are all on a journey, the way of suffering that devo-
tional writer Oswald Chambers describes as "the way of the long,
long trail."[1]

We hope you'll read our words as encouragement to persevere
and to turn the hardships of your lives into something positive. We
pray that you will experience fellowship with Jesus, a Savior who
himself experienced rejection, loneliness, betrayal, and unimaginable physical suffering.

In other words, we're not saying this is easy. We're all afraid to
suffer. We instinctively resist the idea of voluntarily laying down our
lives. We want comfort, a nice, long, prosperous, healthy, peaceful
life surrounded by people who love us. But this dream is not the
vision of life Jesus calls us to.

The Angola Road

Several years ago, Christie and I (Paul) went to Namibia to minister at a Youth for Christ (YFC) camp. We made an agreement that we would come to speak if the Namibia YFC director would drive us north to Angola to visit missionaries from our church who were serving there. The YFC director readily agreed because he hoped to make contact with Angolan leaders who could help start YFC in that country.

The Namibia camp concluded, and we (Christie, the Youth for Christ director, and I) prepared for the journey. Angola had recently ended a long civil war, and we knew the journey would be tough because many of the roads had been destroyed by bombs. We hoped we could visit and offer some encouragement to Christians working in a hospital in the city of Lubango.

Two days before we left, seven British tourists were attacked (including four that were machine-gunned to death) on the road we'd be traveling. As we sat and evaluated whether we should go, our YFC partner said in a decisive, powerful, Paul-the-apostle-like way, "I say let's go! What's the worst that could happen? We'll be killed for Christ and go to glory."

I know I should have agreed, but sometimes I'm a pessimist. I imagined the worst. I replied, "No, the worst that could happen is that we would be captured and tortured for a *really, really, really* long time—and then we might *not* die but rather wither away in prison, and then we'd die and go to glory."

There's nothing like imminent risk of getting shot or captured to help focus the mind. It makes us evaluate our passion and calling. Quoting a phrase attributed to Dr. Martin Luther King Jr., "No one knows why they are alive until they know what they would die for."[2]

After getting some good advice—"Don't drive at night. Stay on this road. If you need to stop by the road and sleep, pull into this police station about half way there"—we decided to embark on our journey. On the first night, the three of us camped out in a police compound, under a Cuban flag, surrounded by a dozen policemen and over two hundred slightly inebriated Cuban soldiers.[3] These soldiers had not seen their wives or girlfriends in a very long time, and my wife was the only female on the compound. I imagined something far worse that night than dying and going to heaven. (Risking my own life is one thing; risking the safety of my loved ones is quite another!)

I confess that, in spite of Jesus' warnings about repetitive prayers, I prayed Psalm 23 about one hundred times that night, focusing specifically on the phrase, "Even though I walk through the valley of death, I will fear no evil."

I am convinced that angels must have blinded the soldiers to our presence because none of them even came near. We made it through the night and to our colleagues in Lubango the next day. God brought us through and deepened our faith, but we had to be willing to put our own lives and each other's at risk. To give a testimony of deliverance, sometimes you need to go through situations that require God to deliver you!

Bottom line: it is never easy to choose sacrifice and risk, hardship and potential suffering.

Hardship, Passion, and Calling

In the classic eighteenth-century biography *The Life of Samuel Johnson*, author James Boswell records one of Johnson's most famous quotations: "Depend upon it, sir, when a man knows he is to be hanged in a fortnight [two weeks], it concentrates his mind wonderfully."[4]

When I tried to sleep in that Angolan police station, my prayers were focused without distraction. The thought of everything those soldiers could do to us concentrated my mind wonderfully!

When Job suffered multiple internal (health) and external (family and wealth) losses, his friends urged him to give up. Job's suffering concentrated his mind on the source of his ultimate hope: "though he slay me, yet will I hope in him" (Job 13:15).

When the disciples heard the toughest saying of Jesus about the suffering that lay ahead, many of them abandoned the mission. Peter didn't fully understand the full extent of Jesus' or their own future sufferings, but he realized he was passionate about Jesus and his teaching: "Lord, to whom shall we go? You have the words of eternal life" (John 6:68).

When Paul writes to the Philippians, he is either in prison or under some sort of house arrest (see Philippians 1:13-14). He realizes that death might be imminent, and his mind concentrates on the passion of his life—"one thing I do"—namely, his overarching passion to know Jesus Christ his Lord (Philippians 3:10). When he writes his second letter to Timothy from prison, Paul knows that his earthly life is soon over. He reflects and states clearly that in the face of death, he has completed his God-given mission, he has finished the race, and his eternal reward is ahead (2 Timothy 4:6-8).

As difficult as our experiences of suffering or hardship might be, God can use them to fuel passion in us and help us discover his unique call on our lives. Ironically, our greatest grief can reveal the greatest gifts we can offer the world. Our suffering is often the surprising generator for our best creative efforts.

Amy Carmichael, missionary to India, allowed her own difficult family background and her later sufferings to be turned into a passion to rescue young girls from temple prostitution.

Mary Slessor, from a hostile and abusive childhood, went to Calabar, southeast Nigeria, and became a pioneer missionary. She turned the pain of her own childhood into a commitment to unwanted children, rescuing twins who were going to be killed because the local cultural legend held that one of the two was a devil.

Joni Eareckson Tada, paralyzed by a diving accident in her teen years, has turned her life-altering injuries into an opportunity to become one of the foremost passionate Christian advocates for people with disabilities.

All of us face this question when we face our personal experiences of suffering or loss: Will we allow God to turn our pain into passion for him and into a specific calling our pain has uniquely prepared us for?

Passion and Calling

What is my core passion? Yours? Passion is the thing that gets us up and keeps us going. The thing that—when we confront it—we conclude, "Yes. This is what I'm living for."[5]

But passion—especially of the long-term zealous variety—is tough to come by in our overchoice world. We might go to the Justice Conference one month and decide we're passionate about combating the human slave trade. Two months later, we read about the destruction of the rain forest and discover our passion for ecology. And in between, a challenging blog has triggered our zeal to get more involved in politics.

Discovering our passion and calling—even through the difficult vehicle of suffering—can help us realize that we can realistically dedicate ourselves to only one or two causes. Our current era is sometimes referred to by social observers as a "passionless" generation, but it might be more a diffused passion across too many options rather than passionlessness. In this pluralistic age we conclude that the operating cultural value seems to be total acceptance of everything and commitment to nothing. The resultant sense of being overwhelmed by too many passions (overchoice) versus apathy (the inner voice that says "What difference could I make, after all?") leads to the conclusion that we live in an "age of indifferentism."

The editors of *Leadership* magazine captured this in a cartoon. The pastor is speaking to a group of adults—obviously calling them to a life of passionate higher commitment and discipleship. A fellow in the back raises his hand and asks, "Pastor, is it possible to *audit* this class on total commitment?"

Many of us live in a culture of nonchalance. Half-heartedness. We fear things like passion because we're so against "obsessive-compulsive behaviors"—yet ironically, every weekend, millions of us sit and passionately watch obsessive-compulsive sports figures passionately battle it out! And passionate fans scream, color their faces, and brave extreme weather in order to support their favorite teams. We've developed the ability to be passionate about things that don't matter while being apathetic about the meaning and purpose of our lives.

What is passion? Before exploring the specifics of refining our passion in order to integrate it with our sense of calling and the redemption of our pain, we need to understand what passion looks like. A dictionary defines *passion* as "fervor, enthusiasm, zeal, an intense emotion compelling action."

The biblical word for passion takes it a step further. The Greek word *paschō* is literally linked to the verb "to suffer," as in Acts 1:3, translated by some as "the passion of Christ." Any reader from a more liturgical tradition understands this connection; the week between Palm Sunday and Easter is Passion Week—the week of the betrayal, trial, suffering, torture, and crucifixion of Jesus Christ.

Combine the dictionary definition with the biblical meaning related to suffering, and we come up with a full understanding of passion: "Passion is love so intense that we'd be willing to suffer or die for it."

This is why we connect passion to the theme of the fellowship of the suffering. In short, there is no pain-free passion. There is no passion lite. There is no such thing as partial passion or half-hearted passion. Passionate people are not simply those who have found something they enjoy doing. Rather, passionate people are those willing to pay the price, absorb the cost, and go after their purposes with sold-out zeal.

A Biblical Picture of Passion

When we think of godly passion, the type we want to rekindle so that we renew our sense of how our hardships could help define God's call on our lives, the picture to consider comes from Paul's letter to the Philippians. Writing from some form of captivity, Paul articulates his passion. In stating his sense of calling, he lists all of the normal things we might cite in a résumé or a biographical sketch—his heritage, his past accomplishments, his training, and his zeal. But he contrasts these against the passion that drives him now.

> But whatever were gains to me I now consider loss for the sake of Christ. What is more, I consider everything a loss because of the surpassing worth of knowing Christ Jesus my Lord, for whose sake I have lost all things. I consider them garbage, that I may gain Christ and be found in him, not having a righteousness of my own that comes from the law, but that which is through faith in Christ—the righteousness that comes from God on the basis of faith. I want to know Christ—yes, to know the power of his resurrection and participation in his sufferings, becoming like him in his death, and so, somehow attaining to the resurrection of the dead.
>
> Not that I have already obtained all this, or have already arrived at my goal, but I press on to take hold of that for which Christ Jesus took hold of me. Brothers and sisters, I do not consider myself yet to have taken hold of it. But one

thing I do: Forgetting what is behind and straining toward what is ahead, I press on toward the goal to win the prize for which God has called me heavenward in Christ Jesus. (Philippians 3:7-14)

Paul, the great evangelist and apostle, obviously serves as an example of one who lived with an overwhelming zeal for ministry and missions, but here he articulates his supreme passion—to know Jesus Christ, both his power and his sufferings. Philippians 3:7-14 stands as a unique proclamation concerning Paul's passion. He writes this letter with some unique vocabulary that sets this portion of the letter apart for his readers and for us. He uses five words that appear only here in the whole Bible:

- *garbage* or *refuse* (v. 8)
- *becoming like him* or *conformed* (v. 10)
- *straining* (v. 13)
- *goal* (v. 14)[6]

Why the unique language? Because Paul wants his readers to sit up and take notice. He's saying something special here. He's articulating his life passion—namely, to know Jesus Christ! Remember, Paul is writing from prison. Pain and suffering concentrate the mind and help us focus on what we really believe in. When he uses the strong word *garbage* (v. 8), he's telling the Philippian readers that all of his former passions (see Philippians 3:4-6) are nothing— rubbish, trash, dung, manure—compared to the surpassing value of knowing Christ.

When he says that he is "forgetting what is behind" (v. 13), he states, "I'm not resting on past laurels, past experiences, past loves." Instead, he's now "straining" for what lies ahead, like a competitive runner lunging across the finish line.

Paul's example confronts us with our own passion. What are we passionate about? Are we passionate to know Christ and to make that the top priority of our lives? Are we like John Bunyan's pilgrim in *Pilgrim's Progress,* who, when lured by the securities and comforts of a dispassionate life, put his fingers in his ears and embarked on his journey shouting "Life, life, eternal life!"?[7] Are we passionate for eternal life—which is to know God and Jesus Christ, who was sent by God (John 17:3)?

Or have we grown cold and complacent, like those in the church at Ephesus in Revelation 2, who forgot their first love? Are we just interested in enough religion to season our life, like spice on our own self-centered existence?

Witness, evangelism, service, and all other forms of a demonstrably Christian lifestyle flow from a passion to know Christ. Out of that passion flows our love for compassionate care of others, our motivation to share the good news of Jesus, and our willingness to grow through our hardships. When we're filled with the love of Christ and understand his love for us, then we overflow and touch the lives of the people around us.

So then the question becomes, How can we kindle or rekindle the fire that burns with the desire to know Jesus Christ? How can we fuel the flame with passionate zeal to know Christ—a flame that makes all other pursuits seem like "garbage" by comparison? How can we turn our prisons into a sense of calling into the world?

Four exercises can help set us on the right path.

Exercise 1: Pray Psalm 86:11

In his zeal to know God, the psalmist prays, "Give me an undivided heart / that I may fear your name" (Psalm 86:11). In other words, Lord, I ask you to focus me, focus my life, and help me stay focused on that which is supposed to be my top priority. The Quakers called this spiritual discipline "centering down"—quieting our hearts to ask Jesus to be the core of our lives.

We know how to quote Philippians 3:13—"one thing I do"—but we often have scattered lives. Some days we're zealous to know Christ, but other days a thousand other interests distract us. Most of these things are not evil—they're just less than the best, which is knowing Jesus Christ.

We can paraphrase Psalm 86:11: "Lord, I'm scattered, distracted, unfocused. Unite my heart. Bring all aspects of my life under the supreme target of knowing Jesus Christ."

When knowing Jesus is truly our top priority, we see our difficulties and hardships through a new lens. We can see that God is making us more identified with Jesus and with his sacrificial work in the world. In contrast, when the focus of our lives is diffused by any number of secondary priorities, going deeper in relationship with Jesus gets squeezed out of our schedules.

Exercise 2: Fuel the Passion

We can fuel the passion to know Christ by getting with passionate-to-know-God people.[8] This is where our fellowship with other passionate sufferers comes into play. I (Paul) recently spent a week of ministry at a fairly rustic camp in Nigeria with Jonathan Lamb from the United Kingdom. Jonathan was a former regional staff person with the International Fellowship of Evangelical Students in Europe. He now travels the world as a Bible expositor. Jonathan suffered polio as a child, leaving one of his legs shorter and malformed. He walks with one or two canes and a specially designed shoe on his left foot. His physical limitation has not kept him from going into the world out of love for Christ and out of commitment to helping students love Christ. His passion to follow Christ in spite of hardships deeply encouraged my own passion to persevere.

This One Thing

Because this has been such a repeated struggle for both of us, I (Dave) crafted a spoken word piece on this passage to help me do the "one thing." Perhaps this can become a helpful prayer for you as well.

This one thing I do
This one thing I think
This one thing I breathe
This one thing, I am
Leaving the rest behind
Out of my sight, out of my mind
Out of my wants, out of my time
For there is no time
You'd think there's room
    for more
But space does not permit for
    even two
That's why it's *this one thing*
    I do
My one thing is you
Not you and this or that or him
    or her
Or here or there, behind
    or before
Not you *plus*
Performance or pleasure
Possessions or popularity
Not you *plus*
Diversions, distractions
Recognitions, rewards
Not you *plus*

Outdoing, outshining
Outlasting, outstanding
Not you *plus*
No, just one thing—you
More and more
Through and through
Inside and out, right and left
Within and about
You, you, you
For there's no need for more
You are all; you are enough
You are everything; you are love
Nothing compares; nothing
    comes close
Only you satisfy, and oh
How my soul *is* satisfied
Yet I long for more, seek more
Thirst and stretch and grasp
And cry out for more
So much more
To taste and see
And be still and know
And live and move and have
All my being wrapped up in
The one thing whose presence
Gives life, brings life
Makes life, is life.
There's one thing I do, because
    there's only one thing *to* do
One thing or nothing
One thing I ask of the Lord, and
    that I will seek:
Just you.

I have had the privilege of knowing George Verwer, founder of Operation Mobilization, over the past three decades. George fuels my passion to know Christ. He is acutely aware of his failures, his personal pain, and his weaknesses, but he has turned all of these things into passion for Jesus. His love for the world and his desire to see people come to know Christ flows from his relationship with Jesus Christ. When my heart grows cold, it always helps me to read something George has written, listen to one of his tapes, or—on a few unique occasions—pray with George personally. His passion ignites mine.

If we want to catch fire with the zeal to know Christ, we need to get with people who are themselves on fire. Their zeal ignites us. We do well to find a friend who helps fuel our fire to know Christ.

What do we do when there's no such person around? If there's no living person who can help you refocus your commitment to know Jesus Christ, then go to the library and find some biographies of Christians who have gone before us. Reading the great stories of people like Jim Elliot, Amy Carmichael, C. T. Studd, Adoniram Judson, or Hudson Taylor (to name only a few) can stir us to imitate their zeal to know Jesus Christ.

Exercise 3: Don't Waste Your Pain

This third exercise designed to rekindle passion to know Christ comes out of Philippians 3:10. Paul writes that he wants to know Christ and the power of his resurrection *and* the fellowship of sharing in his sufferings. All of us want that first part—the power of Christ's resurrection—but few of us want the second—the fellowship of sharing in Christ's sufferings.

Is Paul advocating a spiritual masochism in which we look for opportunities to suffer? Of course not. He's merely stating a theme throughout the Bible: that God uses or allows hardship in our lives to draw us to himself, deepen our character, and intensify our witness.

Clearly, growing through pain is never easy. Our human response to any type of pain—physical, emotional, or social—starts with the prayer, "Lord, please take away the pain." But what do we do when God doesn't take the pain away? Our second prayer should be "Lord, if you're not going to take this pain away, then please use this pain to fuel my desire to know you. Use this pain for your purpose and to fuel my passion. Use this pain to make me more compassionate, to take me to others in pain who need to know your hope in the face of suffering."

Passion is tough because it's connected to pain. But God calls us to imitate Christ, even to the point of allowing our pain to be used for his kingdom. Are we willing to say, "Lord Jesus, I invite you to use my dysfunctional past, my physical pain, my learning disabilities, my emotional pain, my brokenness to fuel passion for you and dedication to your mission in the world"?

Exercise 4: Fight Passion Busters

All of us confront things in our lives that dissipate our passion to know Christ. When we identify these things, we can determine to fight against them. We've identified at least four things that dissolve our passion. Maybe they relate to you. Maybe you have your own list.

Bitterness. Bitterness destroys passion to know Jesus because it takes what could be powerful positive emotional zeal toward Christ and sends it in a negative direction. When we focus on some unresolved hurt in our lives—either toward God or another person—it distracts us from a 100 percent focus on Jesus Christ.

The irony about bitterness is this: although our anger or emotion is directed at someone who has hurt us, *we* end up getting hurt.

Bitterness always exhausts and destroys the one who holds it—not the object of the bitterness.

The challenge is to fuel our passion through ongoing commitment to be a forgiving person.

Security. Desire for security waters down passion. Our addiction to security, safety, and comfort—especially in the affluent world—will almost always overtake that radical commitment that comes from passion. Passion involves risk. Passion involves abandonment of secondary purposes in favor of a supreme goal.

In my mid-forties, I (Paul) had a wonderful position at our church. Good salary. Job security. Opportunities to travel. And a wonderfully affirming climate. But over a two-year period, God let me know it was time to move on to other ministry. I resisted because I didn't want to jump from a comfortable job and secure salary into a world of higher risk and raising support for mission work. I was addicted to my comforts.

Eventually, God helped me gradually release my grip on my comfort-zone living. God had been telling me to move on and entrust my future totally to him, but my desire for security reduced passion for God. I hesitated giving it all up.

Then I read a story in Daniel 3. As the three young friends of Daniel face the fiery furnace of King Nebuchadnezzar, they refuse to succumb to his pressure to bow down and worship him. So he stokes the fire even hotter—to the point that those doing the stoking drop dead. As the three face their own death because of their obedience to God, they tell the king, "The God we serve is able to deliver us." They articulate their faith, but then they state their passion to be God's men by completing the sentence: "*But even if he does not*, we're still not bowing down to you, king."

Their passion to obey God and be true to their relationship with him led them to the inevitable conclusion—security and safety is a secondary issue! I read that story and made up my mind. I'll step out in faith and obey God—whatever it takes!

The challenge is to fuel our passion by the ongoing commitment to life of open-handed release.

Materialism. The third passion-buster we see in ourselves is materialism. As part of our affluent world, we can fall prey to the temptation to live for the pursuit of *stuff*. As we do this, our passion for Christ and his kingdom goes down the drain. Our desire for more and more possessions douses the fire of passion. It means we spend our energies on earning and spending, accumulating and collecting. Our houses are so filled with stuff that we simply have neither the energy nor the time to be 100 percent devoted to knowing Christ Jesus.

The challenge is to fuel our passion through ongoing commitment to a lifestyle of simplicity and contentment.

Fame. The idol of fame causes many of us to draw attention to ourselves rather than to what God ultimately wants us to do. Hardly anything dissolves passion for Christ like obsession over self. Pursuing personal fame—even for Christ—pulls fellowship apart by prioritizing glory over obedience and self-interest over the interest of others. Those who live with genuine passion sacrifice because of love, not because of the possible attention they might receive for doing something great for God.

The challenge is to fuel our passion by the ongoing commitment to a lifestyle of humility characterized by dependency on God.

Conclusion

Everyone shudders a little at the idea of sacrifice. But a passion to imitate Christ's sacrifice always involves dying to ourselves, to our securities, and to our errant expectations about the life of faith. If the fear of sacrifice paralyzes us, we will never go to the poor places, the violent places, and the dangerous places on earth— often the places most lacking in the knowledge of the good news of Jesus Christ.

Without sacrificial, obedient, passionate risk-takers for Jesus Christ, who will reach the gangs of the cities, the impoverished, those dying of preventable diseases, the terrorists? Without passion to imitate Jesus, where will we find courage to be witnesses where God has placed us? Or to make the great economic sacrifices necessary to expand the kingdom of Christ?

What does this passion to imitate Jesus Christ look like?

- It's people making themselves available to God—without reservation—whatever it takes!

- It's risk-taking faith, stepping out—not recklessly but without knowing how God will deliver us.

- It's coming together in community to encourage each other to make the sacrifices necessary to best serve the global purposes of God.

- It means perseverance. An emotional response is not enough. Sacrifice is sticking with it, not being swayed by the voices of comfort or convenience, not being distracted from the process God is leading us on.

In *Walking with God through Pain and Suffering*, Tim Keller describes the climatic point in operas called the aria. The aria is when a leading character enters into all the tragedy of the story and situation, embraces and embodies the pain himself, and turns it into a beautiful song. Characters are reluctant to do this because of the burden, uncertainty, and tension of the situation. Even the audience would like to bypass this part and jump to the resolution. But the aria brings the beauty out of the tragedy, the hope out of the disappointment, the strength out of the weakness, the passion out of the pain.[9]

Ultimately, Jesus sings the aria for us. He steps into all the brokenness, lostness, and suffering of our world, and brings life to the dying, hope to the hurting, and strength to the failing. The cross is the most beautiful song of passionate love ever sung. Just as Jesus sings the aria for us, we must sing it for others by coming alongside and sharing their suffering, entering into the hurt and heartache, and with Christ, striving to turn it into something beautiful. This is to be our song. This is how suffering is overcome.

Suffering comes with the territory because suffering refines us, reshapes us, and helps us discover and release our hearts' ultimate passion—Jesus.

Forging Fellowship Reflections

1. Which of the "passion busters" might affect you most? Why?

2. How can Christians fuel passion to know Jesus in ourselves and in our fellowships?

3. If passion is loving something so intently that you'd be willing to suffer or die for it, what's your passion?

Epilogue

All pain's a prelude: to symphony, to sweetness.

EUGENE PETERSON, *HOLY LUCK*

OUR INTENT THROUGHOUT THIS BOOK has been to encourage those who suffer to live as fully and faithfully as possible. The primary way we can do this is to accept suffering's unexpected invitation: fellowship. Suffering opens the doors of possibility for us to experience deeper fellowship with God, closer fellowship with others, and wider fellowship with our beautiful but broken world.

We can experience deeper fellowship with God through suffering first by praying through our suffering. Suffering comes with the territory of following Christ, and prayer is suffering's best result. Second, suffering can have a powerfully transformative effect on our character, because hardship is a crucible in which Christlikeness can be richly cultivated. The more we become like Christ, the more communion we will experience with God. Finally, pain, when shared with Jesus, can birth within us a joy that cannot be broken. We believe the world so desperately hungers for this kind of joy. It cannot be found apart from Christ, and it cannot be found in Christ apart from pain.

Not only does suffering deepen our fellowship with Christ, but it can enable us to forge closer fellowship with others. More than anything else, what birthed our (Dave and Paul) growing friendship and partnership in ministry has been the suffering we have been able to share with one another. Not only do we believe fellowship like this is possible for us but also for all who desire to follow Jesus together. Community often blooms most beautifully out of grounds of shared suffering. The examples of our brothers and sisters like Elisabeth and Jim Elliot, Eugene and Jan Peterson, Adoniram Judson, Amy Carmichael, the martyrs of Sudan, and "the great cloud of witnesses" teach us this. Not only that, but they invite us to suffer faithfully. Together this fellowship of the suffering is able to bear witness to the suffering Christ in ways that cannot be done otherwise.

Our prayer for God's global church is that it would become famous for being a fellowship of the suffering. When those who are living apart from God experience suffering, as they inevitably will, our hope is that they would seek solace from those who best know how to suffer. Because of Jesus, we have every reason to be this kind of people. May God use all of our pain to enable us to find common ground with those who are hurting, so they in turn might experience the power and healing and life found in fellowship with our resurrected King.

As the church lives into its calling to be a fellowship of the suffering, opportunities arise for us to widen our fellowship with our pain-stricken world. We have strived to demonstrate throughout this book *the suffering caused by evil is overcome by the suffering inspired by cross-like love*. The suffering human community has the potential to be gradually healed through connection to a fellowship of sufferers experiencing healing through fellowship with our Lord Jesus Christ, the suffering Servant. Our collective willingness to "fill up in the flesh what is lacking in Christ's afflictions" enables God's kingdom to advance through our missional endeavors at home, at work, and around the world. Our willingness to faithfully suffer with Christ, like Christ, and out of passionate love for Christ is how the transformative power of Christianity is most fully unleashed for the good of the world. Thus, we need to regularly ask ourselves, How might God be calling me to *passionately* follow him today?

The End of Suffering

While this call to suffer faithfully is necessary now, it won't be forever. Revelation 21–22 provides us with the picture of the future reality where suffering will be no more. We are given the unquenchable promise that God "will wipe away every tear from their eyes, and death shall be no more, neither shall there be mourning, nor crying, nor pain anymore, for the former things have passed away" (Revelation 21:4 ESV).

Suffering is a *former thing*, not a *permanent thing*. If suffering has a beginning (Genesis 3), then suffering must also have an ending. Thus we can fully and fearlessly proclaim with the apostle Paul, "I consider that the sufferings of this present time are not worth comparing with the glory that is to be revealed to us" (Romans 8:18 ESV).

The time is *now* for the church to become a fellowship of the suffering. Still, we can and must look expectantly toward the day when all suffering will be redeemed, and we instead will be transfigured into "a fellowship of glory." While God has mysteriously allowed suffering to make an entrance into this world, we are assured that one day it will be given a permanent exit. Until then, we must join together with Christ, and fellow believers near and far, past, present, and future, in entering the world's deep suffering in every place and every person.

To help us in this urgent task, we have crafted a *declaration* for all those who desire to be a part of the fellowship of the suffering to profess their intent. While being a part of this fellowship is undoubtedly communal in nature, we've written this from the individual standpoint, because none of us will be able to live as fully and faithfully as possible unless we regularly make the *personal* commitment to do so. We encourage you to place this declaration where you can read it and pray through it often, lest any of us drift away from this all-important mission.

I am a part of the fellowship of the suffering
I follow Christ not simply to be saved
or to know just the power of the empty grave
but to live out all his ways
not just when it feels good on Sundays
but when it hurts, when it's hard, like on Good Friday
For without this day his message of love could never
     get across
Because his message of love is a cross
Thus to follow Christ is to share in his sufferings
the suffering that made a covering for sin
so that all that has been
might no longer be
but that all might step into the reality
of what Christ calls eternity
While the offer is free
the price is high
Which is why when Christ calls us
he bids us come and die
To live is Christ and to die is gain
Dying means denying
my comforts, my fears, my ambitions, my wants
Dying means defying
the ways of the world, the flesh and the devil
Dying means crying
over the injustices of those who go without, and our
     personal pain within

Dying means unifying
to come together, share burdens, alleviate ache through our
    own heartbreak
all with Jesus, for his kingdom's sake
Dying means crucifying
like bread and wine, being broken, poured out, and given
so that every person on the planet could be made whole,
    filled, and truly start living
I am part of the fellowship of the suffering
But I am far from alone
I stand on the shoulders of the giants of past
the global church of the present
and the generations being raised up for the future
until Christ comes again
But I don't have to wait for his return
to begin to learn
how Christ might live if he was me
For he's shown that the way to life will inevitably
lead up the hill called Calvary
For it is there in his woundedness and our own
that suffering is overcome by suffering
and Jesus is truly, intimately, and most fully known
We are a part of the fellowship of the suffering.

Acknowledgments

THROUGH OUR MANY combined years of serving as pastors and leaders, we've seen some remarkable people responding courageously to some very dramatic challenges and hardships—from overseas colleagues who have been imprisoned and suffered greatly for their faith to local parents who have suffered the loss of a child to cancer, a car accident, or even suicide. We have had the privilege of standing in the fellowship of the suffering with hurting people at a hospital bedside or an open graveside. These friends have invited us to share their sorrows, and their responses have shaped our characters and our understanding of God's grace.

The names are too many to list—because some may prefer their privacy, but mostly because we fear leaving someone out. But we do want to acknowledge specifically our Grace Chapel family and staff, our team in Development Associates International, our spiritual directors and counselors, our families, and our faithful friends who have loved us through our toughest times. We want to give a special word of thanks to our InterVarsity Press editor, Al Hsu, who not only makes us better writers but shared his own story and invited us into his suffering.[1]

But through all of our adult years, our greatest partners in the fellowship of suffering, loss, challenge, and hardship have been our wives. I (Paul) gratefully dedicate this book to Christie, fellow pilgrim for almost four decades. I (Dave) dedicate this book to Erin—I count it all joy.

Recommended Reading

HERE ARE A FEW BOOKS that have helped us most in trying to understand the role of suffering and hardship in the life and ministry of Christians.

Broken and Whole by Stephen A. Macchia
The Broken Way by Ann Voskamp
The Cost of Discipleship by Dietrich Bonhoeffer
Five Smooth Stones for Pastoral Work by Eugene Peterson
A Grace Disguised by Jerry Sittser
A Path Through Suffering by Elisabeth Elliot
Walking with God Through Pain and Suffering by Tim Keller
Where Is God When It Hurts? and *Disappointment with God* by
    Philip Yancey
The Wounded Healer by Henri Nouwen

Notes

Preface

[1]Two lines in this piece are quotations. "You cannot go around a desert" is from Christian Wiman, *My Bright Abyss* (New York: Farrar, Straus, & Giroux, 2013), 140. "Where the sufferer is, there God is" is taken from Eugene Peterson, *Five Smooth Stones for Pastoral Work* (Grand Rapids: Eerdmans, 1992), 114.

1 Suffering Comes with the Territory

[1]While I was a student in seminary, I had the privilege of meeting Elisabeth's mother, Katherine Howard. Through Mrs. Howard I eventually met Mrs. Elliot personally, and I later took a seminary course with her.

[2]See Elisabeth Elliot's books *Through Gates of Splendor,* 50th anniv. ed. (Wheaton, IL: Tyndale Momentum, 1981), and *Shadow of the Almighty,* rev. ed. (New York: HarperCollins, 2009), which describe both Jim's passion and the account of the Auca encounter.

[3]Described in her book *The Savage My Kinsman*, 40th anniv. ed. (Ventura, CA: Regal, 2003).

[4]Many of the other books written by Elisabeth Elliot build on this idea of suffering as part of the Christian experience. These books include *Discipline: The Glad Surrender*; *On Asking God Why*; *Love Has a Price Tag*; *A Path Through Suffering: Discovering the Relationship Between God's Mercy and Our Pain*; *A Chance to Die: The Life and Legacy of Amy Carmichael*; *Facing the Death of Someone You Love* (booklet); and *The Path of Loneliness.*

[5]Elisabeth Elliot, *A Path Through Suffering* (Ann Arbor, MI: Servant, 1990), 56.

[6]J. Schattenmann, "Fellowship," in *New International Dictionary of New Testament Theology*, ed. Colin Brown (Grand Rapids: Zondervan, 1986), 1:643.

⁷This phrase comes from the title of Steve Corbett and Brian Fikkert's book *When Helping Hurts* (Chicago: Moody Publishers, 2009).

⁸Scott J. Hafemann, "Suffering," in *Dictionary of Paul and His Letters,* ed. Gerald Hawthorne and Ralph Martin (Downers Grove, IL: IVP Academic, 1993), 920.

⁹John R. W. Stott, *The Cross of Christ* (Downers Grove, IL: InterVarsity Press, 2006), 313.

¹⁰Dietrich Bonhoeffer, *The Cost of Discipleship* (New York: Touchstone, 1995), 92; italics added.

2 The Worst Suffering: Paul's Story

¹On the cross, Jesus not only articulated his physical (thirst) and emotional (why have you forsaken me) pain, he also offered forgiveness to the repentant thief, looked to the care of his mother, and prayed forgiveness on his persecutors (Matthew 27:26; Mark 15:34; Luke 23:34, 43, 46; John 19:26-30).

²Some of our sufferings are caused by accidents, disasters, or other people. But some may be at least partly due to unwise behaviors: sitting unprotected in the sun and getting skin cancer; smoking cigarettes and getting COPD or lung cancer; riding a bike or a motorcycle without a helmet. But thankfully God's mercy still prevails over even this suffering. By his grace, he can use these maladies to do something good long-term in us and through us.

³Generally speaking, prosperity theology teaches that God's desired outcome for the Christian life of faith is financial, physical, and even relational wealth. Its fundamental contention is that if we love God enough, give enough, do enough, then God will bless us with health, wealth, and material prosperity, not merely in the life to come but now. Suffering, trial, and hardship have no place in the Christian life. They're only hurdles God might set before us to help propel us into greater blessing. (This sometimes is true, but in no way should it be taught as the prescribed norm.)

3 Learning to Trust Anyway: Dave and Erin's Story

¹"Orphans," UNICEF, updated June 16, 2017, www.unicef.org/media/media_45279.html.

²Timothy Keller with Katherine Leary Alsdorf, *Every Good Endeavor: Connecting Your Work to God's Work* (New York: Dutton, 2012), 29.

[3]Jerry Sittser, *A Grace Disguised,* exp. ed. (Grand Rapids: Zondervan, 2004), 17.

[4]Eugene Peterson, *Five Smooth Stones for Pastoral Work* (Grand Rapids: Eerdmans, 1992), 114.

4 The Sun Comes from the Dark: Prayer Through Suffering

[1]Abraham Joshua Heschel, quoted in Eugene Peterson, *Five Smooth Stones for Pastoral Work* (Grand Rapids: Eerdmans, 1992), 133.

[2]The title of this chapter, "The Sun Comes from the Dark," is a phrase from Wendell Berry, *This Day* (Berkeley: Counterpoint, 2013), 207.

[3]Peterson, *Five Smooth Stones*, 132.

[4]Blaise Pascal, quoted in Philip Yancey, *Where Is God When It Hurts?* (Grand Rapids: Zondervan, 1990), 114.

[5]If you'd like to picture more clearly what I'm referring to, or if you feel tempted to purchase one of these beanbags for yourself, check out yogibo.com. In all seriousness, if you struggle to be still, it might be one of the best investments you make for your prayer life.

[6]Timothy Keller, *Prayer* (New York: Dutton, 2014), 48.

[7]Timothy Keller, *Walking with God Through Pain and Suffering* (New York: Penguin, 2015), 5.

[8]Keller, *Prayer*, 228.

[9]Peterson, *Five Smooth Stones*, 118.

[10]"Walking with Grief," *Celtic Book of Daily Prayer* (New York: HarperOne, 2002), 225.

[11]For a fuller yet accessible treatment on Ignatian contemplation, see James Martin, *The Jesuit Guide to (Almost) Everything: A Spirituality for Real Life* (New York: HarperCollins, 2012), 145-50.

[12]This sequence of prayer was inspired by John Baillie's fine work, *A Diary of Private Prayer* (New York: Fireside, 1949), 71.

[13]Dietrich Bonhoeffer, *Life Together* (New York: Harper & Row, 1954), 86.

[14]The previous six paragraphs were adapted from Paul Borthwick, "Empathetic Praying," in *Rev!*, January-February 2004, 26.

5 Becoming the Kind of People the World Needs: Transformation Through Suffering

[1]Philip Yancey and Paul Brand, *Pain: The Gift Nobody Wants* (Grand Rapids: Zondervan, 1993), 12.

[2]This section is adapted from Paul Borthwick, "When Pain Is Your Prison," *Discipleship Journal* 139 (March-April, 2004): 34-39.

[3]Viktor E. Frankl, *Man's Search for Meaning* (Boston: Beacon, 1992), 75; italics added.

[4]The testimony of Stephen appears in Acts 7, but Acts 8 begins with the brief statement that Saul of Tarsus was, in effect, the supervisor of the execution. Perhaps the writer Luke included this because he knew Saul (who in Acts 9 is dramatically converted to Jesus Christ and is renamed Paul, and later Paul, the apostle). Perhaps Stephen's faithful testimony planted the seed of the gospel in Saul while also showing him that suffering would be part of his life after he chose to follow Jesus.

[5]In the book of Philippians, Paul uses the word we translate "joy" or "rejoice" fifteen times—including the phrase "Rejoice in the Lord always. I will say it again: Rejoice!" (4:4). We must remember that Paul wrote these words from some sort of captivity—either a prison cell or chained to a Roman guard under house arrest (Philippians 1:13-14).

[6]This section is adapted from Paul Borthwick, "Living with Chronic Pain," Development Associates International, accessed December 1, 2107, www.daintl.org/wp-content/uploads/2015/05/Chronic-Pain-Paul-Borthwick-v2.pdf.

[7]See Joni's website, Joni and Friends, www.joniandfriends.org.

[8]E. Stanley Jones, *The Divine Yes* (Nashville: Abingdon Press, 1975), 127.

[9]Paul Tournier, *Creative Suffering* (New York: Harper & Row, 1981), 2-3.

[10]This section is adapted from Borthwick, "When Pain Is Your Prison," 37.

[11]Richard Foster, *Celebration of Discipline* (New York: HarperOne, 1978), 1.

[12]For more on how spiritual disciplines can transform us, see Dallas Willard, *The Spirit of the Disciplines* (San Francisco: HarperOne, 1999).

[13]John Henry Jowett, quoted in Gary Inrig, A *Call to Excellence* (Wheaton, IL: Victor Books, 1985), 51.

[14]These thoughts are adapted from an article that originally appeared in *Discipleship Journal*, July-August 2000, 49.

6 Not What I Expected: Joy Through Suffering

[1]Elisabeth Elliot, *A Path Through Suffering* (Ann Arbor, MI: Servant, 1990), 85; italics added.

[2]Eugene Peterson translates it this way: "Celebrate God all day, every day. I mean *revel* in him" (*The Message*).

[3]Ajith Fernando, *The Call to Joy and Pain: Embracing Suffering in Your Ministry* (Wheaton IL: Crossway, 2007), 17, 19.

[4]Dallas Willard, *Living in Christ's Presence* (Downers Grove, IL: InterVarsity Press, 2014), 78.

[5]Eugene Peterson, *A Long Obedience in the Same Direction* (Downers Grove, IL: InterVarsity Press, 2000), 100-101.

[6]Stuart Briscoe, *Bound for Joy* (Glendale, CA: Gospel Light, 1975), 135-36.

[7]Fernando, *Call to Joy and Pain*, 54.

[8]Joni Eareckson Tada, "The Beyond Suffering Bible: An Interview with Joni Eareckson Tada," interview by Jonathan Petersen, BibleGateway Blog, July 14, 2016, www.biblegateway.com/blog/2016/07/the-beyond -suffering-bible-an-interview-with-joni-eareckson-tada.

7 It's Our Family: Solidarity Through Suffering

[1]Elisabeth Elliot, *A Path Through Suffering* (Ann Arbor, MI: Servant, 1990), 66.

[2]Karen Ellis, "From Enemy of the People to Friend," *Christianity Today,* November 2016, 30.

[3]We also reflect on this passage in chapter 8, "Pain as Common Ground."

[4]William Barclay, *The Letters to the Philippians, Colossians and Thessalonians* (Louisville, KY: Westminster Press, 1975), 63.

[5]Ibid., 64.

[6]Amy Carmichael, "No Scar?," in *Toward Jerusalem* (Fort Washington, PA: Christian Literature Crusade, 2013), 85.

[7]See the Center for the Study of Global Christianity website at www .globalchristianity.org. This figure includes people from within all of global Christianity, including Catholics, Orthodox, Anglicans, Protestants, and independents.

[8]Brooke Sulahian, "Our Story," Hope for Our Sisters, accessed October 18, 2017, http://hopeforoursisters.org/about-hope-sisters-fistula-mission-surgeries/story-founding-sisters.

8 Pain as Common Ground: Neighboring Through Suffering

[1]If you'd like to explore this particular question in greater depth, we recommend Jeanette Yep, Peter Cha, Susan Cho Van Riesen, Greg Jao, and Paul Tokunaga, *Following Jesus Without Dishonoring Your Parents* (Downers Grove, IL: InterVarsity Press, 2009).

[2]This section was adapted from Paul Borthwick, "Evangelistic Suffering," *Rev!*, September-October 2003, 29.

[3]Just to be clear, I don't place any particular blame for this way of life on anyone in particular. This was just the general cultural ethos of our blue-collar, Rust Belt community. This was our *normal*. And everyone was expected to act *normally*!

9 The Seed Must Die to Multiply: Mission Through Suffering

[1]John R. W. Stott, *The Cross of Christ* (Downers Grove, IL: InterVarsity Press, 2006), 313.

[2]The Greek word for "witness" in Acts 1:8 ("You will be my witnesses") is *martyria*, the same word from which we get *martyr*. In short, those first-century witnesses knew that bold proclamation of Jesus might cost them their lives.

[3]See John Foxe and Harold J. Chadwick, *The New Foxe's Book of Martyrs* (Newbury, FL: Bridge-Logos, 1997); Lian Xi, *Redeemed by Fire* (New Haven, CT: Yale University Press, 2010); and James and Marti Hefley, *By Their Blood: Christian Martyrs of the Twentieth Century* (Grand Rapids: Baker, 1996).

[4]Ajith Fernando, *The Call to Joy and Pain: Embracing Suffering in Your Ministry* (Wheaton, IL: Crossway, 2007), 85.

[5]Elisabeth Elliot, *A Path Through Suffering* (Ann Arbor, MI: Servant, 1990), 67.

[6]Evans Burns, "The Missionary Life: No Shortcuts," Gospel Coalition, December 5, 2014, www.thegospelcoalition.org/article/the-missionary-life-no-shortcuts.

[7]Helen Roseveare, quoted in Justin Taylor, "A Woman of Whom the World Was Not Worthy: Helen Roseveare (1925-2016)," Gospel Coalition, December 7, 2016, https://blogs.thegospelcoalition.org/

justintaylor/2016/12/07/a-woman-of-whom-the-world-was-not
-worthy-helen-roseveare-1925-2016. Helen's talk can be found at:
https://s3.amazonaws.com/urbana.org/general_session_audio
/urbana-76-helen.roseveare-cost.of.declaring.his.glory.mp3.

[8]Vivian Fernandes and Paul Cornelius, quoted in Jeremy Weber,
"Outpacing Persecution: Why It's the Best of Times and the Worst
of Times for India's Burgeoning Churches," *Christianity Today,* November 2016, 43-44.

[9]G. Campbell Morgan, quoted in Stott, *Cross of Christ,* 351.

[10]This section, including "Chronology of Adoniram Judson's Loss"
and beyond, is adapted from Paul Borthwick, "Endurance Personified in the Life of Judson," *Mission Frontiers*, May 1, 2012, www
.missionfrontiers.org/issue/article/endurance-personified-in-the
-life-of-judson.

[11]Adoniram Judson, quoted in Courtney Anderson, *To the Golden
Shore* (Valley Forge, PA: Judson Press, 1987), 83.

[12]Ibid.

10 Are You Really Passionate? Calling Through Suffering

[1]Oswald Chambers, *My Utmost for His Highest* (London: Marshall,
Morgan & Scott, 1927), 310. The whole statement is: "God's way is
always the way of suffering—the way of the 'long, long trail.'"

[2]Martin Luther King Jr., "Martin Luther King Quotes," *International
Business Times*, January 19, 2015, www.ibtimes.com/martin-luther
-king-quotes-21-memorable-sayings-mlk-day-2015-1783820.

[3]Cuba had sent soldiers to fight alongside the revolutionaries during
the Angolan Civil War (1975–2002).

[4]Samuel Johnson, quoted in "Hanging—It Concentrates the Mind
Wonderfully," *This Day in Quotes*, September 19, 2014, www.this
dayinquotes.com/2009/09/hanging-it-concentrates-mind.html.

[5]The material on the next few pages is adapted from Paul Borthwick,
Stop Witnessing . . . and Start Loving (Colorado Springs: NavPress,
2003), 17-30.

[6]See Sakae Kubo, *A Reader's Greek-English Lexicon of the New
Testament* (Grand Rapids: Zondervan, 1975), 191.

[7]John Bunyan, *Pilgrim's Progress* (Chicago: Moody Press, n.d.), 8.

[8]The material from here to the conclusion is adapted from Borthwick,
Stop Witnessing . . . and Start Loving, 17-30.

[9]Timothy Keller, *Walking with God Through Pain and Suffering* (New York: Penguin, 2015), 165.

Acknowledgments

[1]See Al's book *Grieving a Suicide: A Loved One's Search for Comfort, Answers, and Hope,* rev. ed. (Downers Grove, IL: InterVarsity Press, 2017).

Connect with us online at

fellowshipofthesuffering.com

*Share quotes and other thoughts from the book
on Twitter at*

#FellowshipOfTheSuffering

Other Books by Paul Borthwick

**Great Commission,
Great Compassion**
978-0-8308-4437-1

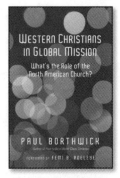

**Western Christians in
Global Mission**
978-0-8308-3780-9

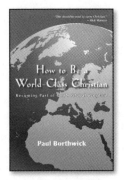

**How to Be a
World-Class Christian**
978-0-8308-5680-0

**Six Dangerous Questions to
Transform Your View of the World**
978-0-8308-1685-9

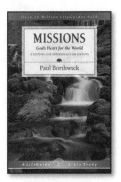

Missions (LBS)
978-0-8308-3090-9

Joseph (LBS)
978-0-8308-3049-7